D0090256

"In a world where we've forgotten how to talk to one another, this book offers an essential blueprint for life-changing conversations. Whether you want to bring people out of their comfort zone or find common ground at the dinner table, Dust's inspired stories and generous wisdom will help you transform ordinary interactions into moments of connection, creativity, and joy."

—Ingrid Fetell Lee, author of *Joyful* and
founder of the Aesthetics of Joy

"It is impossible for anyone to read this book without being moved to try to craft and embark on those 'conversations of our lives'—the ones that we always mean to have, the ones we *need* to have, but somehow the ones we never get to. In a world where genuine communication seems more essential and yet more elusive than ever, Dust's book is the needed spark—personally, organizationally, professionally, politically, and spiritually."

—Mary C. Gentile, PhD, author of *Giving Voice to Values:
How Speak Your Mind When You Know What's Right* and
creator-director of Giving Voice to Values, University of Virginia
Darden School of Business, www.GivingVoiceToValues.org

"Fred Dust has helped some of the world's most powerful people have more productive conversations, and reading this book feels like being engaged in a direct conversation with him. Drawing on his fascinating experiences as a senior leader at IDEO, his design thinking expertise, and his architecture background, he offers actionable advice on how we can all stop talking past each other."

—Adam Grant, *New York Times* bestselling author of *Give and
Take* and *Originals* and host of the TED podcast *WorkLife*

"For decades I have watched Fred design with an eye for what is needed in the future. He has done it again with *Making Conversations* in helping us design our very hardest conversations—the ones we need to provoke real change."

—David Kelley, founder of IDEO and the Stanford d.school

"Improving the state of the world depends on conversations that bridge divides, create solutions, and drive action. The stakes are high for having the best conversations possible, but we leave conversation to instinct, not technique. The foundation has been working with the practices of Fred's book since the early days of 2020. Fred has continuously helped us craft more effective conversations with his easy-to-apply practices. This brilliant book is required reading for anyone who talks to anyone."

—Zia Khan, senior vice president for innovation at the Rockefeller Foundation

"I greatly appreciate Fred's keen intellect and, frankly, just the fun of working with him. His book on how to rethink the hardest conversations in the world personally captures what it is like to work alongside a person whom I now consider a friend."

—Jonathan McBride, former director of the presidential personnel office under Barack Obama

"In this timely and hopeful book, Fred Dust makes the compelling case that revitalizing dialogue is the key to addressing the alienation and polarization of the modern world. *Making Conversation* is essential reading for those looking to enrich their relationships and build community."

—Vivek Murthy, nineteenth surgeon general of the United States

"While I've been fortunate to see Fred's work on conversation and dialogue firsthand, I was moved to see how much of his practice connects back to things from his childhood: Storytelling from his grandparents. Listening from his mother. It's clear he's been doing this work his entire life."

—Jacqueline Novogratz, CEO of Acumen

"Making conversations work is at the heart of living well, personally and professionally. It's what connects us to ourselves and others at every level, what makes us strong through diverse ideas, and what builds solidarity and compassion in uncertain times. Fred Dust has produced the right book at the right time."

—The Right Reverend June Osborne, bishop of Llandaff

"This book offers guidance for having the most productive and engaged conversations as we move forward in a world that desperately needs them. Smart, grounded in deep experience, and immediately useful for our moment, Dust's book insists on this: Have the conversations that count."

—Sherry Turkle, professor of the social studies of science and technology, MIT, and author of *Reclaiming Conversation: The Power of Talk in a Digital Age*

MAKING CONVERSATION

MAKING CONVERSATION

Seven Essential Elements of Meaningful Communication

FRED DUST

HARPER
BUSINESS

An Imprint of HarperCollins*Publishers*

HarperCollins books may be purchased for educational, business, or sales promotional use. For information, please email the Special Markets Department at SPsales@harpercollins.com.

FIRST EDITION

Designed by Nancy Singer

Library of Congress Cataloging-in-Publication Data
Names: Dust, Fred, author.
Title: Making conversation: seven essential elements of meaningful communication / Fred Dust.
Description: New York: Harper Business, 2020. | Includes bibliographical references. | Summary: "A book about how to design meetings and conversations to be more creative and impactful"—Provided by publisher.
Identifiers: LCCN 2020017947 (print) | LCCN 2020017948 (ebook) | ISBN 9780062933904 (hardcover) | ISBN 9780062933911 (ebook)
Subjects: LCSH: Creative ability—Social aspects. | Communication and the arts. | Business communication.
Classification: LCC BF408.D877 2020 (print) | LCC BF408 (ebook) | DDC 302.34/6—dc23
LC record available at https://lccn.loc.gov/2020017947
LC ebook record available at https://lccn.loc.gov/2020017948

---

20 21 22 23 24 LSC 10 9 8 7 6 5 4 3 2 1

For my husband, David, who had to make a lot
of conversations to make this happen

CONTENTS

INTRODUCTION 1

CHAPTER 1 COMMITMENT 21

CHAPTER 2 CREATIVE LISTENING 43

CHAPTER 3 CLARITY 77

CHAPTER 4 CONTEXT 107

CHAPTER 5 CONSTRAINTS 145

CHAPTER 6 CHANGE 173

CHAPTER 7 CREATE 201

ACKNOWLEDGMENTS 225

NOTES 229

MAKING
CONVERSATION

INTRODUCTION

Nowadays, everyone I meet—friends and colleagues, even strangers at dinner parties—keeps asking me some variation of the same question: "I had this conversation today and it just didn't work. What do you think I did wrong?"

The headmaster of a school wondering how she could better handle hard conversations with the powerful and wealthy parents of her students. A CEO trying to navigate decisiveness with prudence. A mother in anguish because her daughter's anorexia has turned the family dinner table into a war zone. A board meeting that went wrong over a single word. A senior member of a police force struggling to talk with her officers about ethics.

Without intending to, I've become a kind of expert in the design of conversations.

Constructive conversation is one of humanity's first and most powerful tools. Conversations built our first communities and helped emerging civilization progress. Public discourse was the foundation of democracy and has been the underpinning of all aspects of government and governance throughout history. And whatever we may feel about our handheld devices and pinging social media accounts, technological "progress" arose from constructive conversations. Creative collaboration was what put humans on the moon and what still keeps us in the digital ether.

But lately it seems like we've all lost the ability to talk to one another. To have productive conversations. To exchange ideas and together advance those ideas.

Everything's moving too fast. The news media promotes friction and faction. Politics and democratic dialogue seem lost to us, each day hitting a new low. College campuses have become so divided by race, class, and gender politics that institutions that were built on dialogue are now afraid to host it at all. Once, we might have believed others were wrong; today, we believe others are lying.

Meanwhile, our children are being driven inward, only able to communicate through their devices, and what we perceive through social media is only the thinnest slice of who we are as humans. The "discourse" online is between figments of ourselves, ghosts in dialogue. We've lost our sense of humanness and it's reflected in the viciousness of the rhetoric that surrounds social media "conversation" today.

This same media system exposes us to such constant tragedy—hurricanes, fires, school shootings, police violence, pandemics, detention camps—that we can't pause and deal with any of them anymore. We simply let these atrocities pile up; we live in perpetual crisis.

Sure, we've always had a hard time having important conversations across political, socioeconomic, gender, or racial lines. But now we're having trouble talking to the people closest to us. It's happening between friends, family, coworkers, people who share political beliefs and goals. The rift is visible everywhere.

For my entire career, I've built my life around the idea that a fresh and creative approach to conversations that matter could save us. Could change the world. But over the last couple of years I found myself in increasing despair. I wasn't sure I actually believed in the power of creative conversation anymore. It was akin to a loss of faith.

How I Became a Designer of Conversation

It all began in 1988 when I dropped out of college to go and work with the HIV activist group ACT UP (AIDS Coalition to Unleash Power).

The early days of ACT UP felt like a creative revolution. So many of those who found themselves afflicted with the disease were artists, playwrights, and designers; their approach to public protest was so fresh and transgressive that a movement about death felt vibrantly alive. The die-ins. The slogan Silence = Death. The reappropriation of the pink triangle—a remnant from the Nazi-era branding of the gay men and women sent to the concentration camps. It was new and modern, and the combination of activist methods and creative coalitions reinvented the landscape of modern protest.

At first, it really was exhilarating: there I was, sitting on the floor of Seattle's Capitol Hill community center, among men and women, gay and straight, artists and laypeople, helping plan the elaborately staged interventions the organization was known for. As the weeks went by, however, it began to feel like there was more time spent planning than doing, more rhetoric than exuberant creativity. I began to feel frustrated with spray-painting signs in Seattle basements and gathering in small group demonstrations that were frankly easy to ignore.

Had my timing been different—a few years earlier and a couple of thousand miles eastward—I may have witnessed something different. The truth was, joining the Seattle chapter of ACT UP had put me in the very outer rings of the burning center. But the deeper and sadder truth was that even that central fire seemed to be flickering and fading. The creative center of artists, writers, performers, and advertising people was literally dying out, hit hard by late-stage HIV. I was in the cold, rainy Seattle streets surrounded not by creative warmth but by a cold anger and a community now mostly defined by their mourning.

But that was the beginning of a journey for me. I was chasing something. I could see the way art and social change could merge—how hard conversations could become both more provocative and more positive through the introduction of creative practice. At the same time, I was watching political conversations on a national and global scale begin to falter and fail. I was trying to balance what seemed an emerging cynicism in the world with the more hopeful practices I believed possible.

A year later I returned to school and shifted my study from politics (I'd once planned to spend a semester working with guerrilla soldiers in Zimbabwe) to art and art history. While the medium was different, the underlying current of what I was engaged with was the same. I chose to study the long history of artists who had made social change through their work. I was looking for the places where art and activism blended together.

My timing couldn't have been better. The work of ACT UP and the political moment were giving rise to artists who were integrating art and politics in all-new ways. In school, I did my thesis work on Barbara Kruger. Her iconic poster for the pro-choice movement, "Your body is a battleground," was known to all. And she was not alone.

After I graduated, I began working with artist activists like Yolanda Lopez and the art collective Border Arts Workshop, who did politically charged work about immigration in California; Mary Kelly, who became notorious for documenting every aspect of her child's first year of life and attracted outsize anger from the mostly male world of art critics; James Luna, a Native American performance artist who put his naked body on display in glass cases in the anthropological wings of museums like the Met; and HIV-positive performance artist Tim Miller, who was known for the confrontationally sexual content of his work. Their art was courageous, clever, witty, and beautiful, but also capable of inspiring bold change. It was encouraging new forms of conversation in the world.

This political moment in the art world coincided with the emergence of new technologies like CD-ROMs—yes, really—and the first skeletal structures of the internet. It was an oddly utopian moment. In fact, the first book I co-edited, *Clicking In: Hot Links to a Digital Culture*, was a collection of exuberant essays by artists celebrating the way new technologies would liberate our identities. Ironically, many of the artists and philosophers in that book, most notably Jaron Lanier, have since embraced a dystopian view of the technologies they once boosted. Later, in the 1990s, the art market exploded, and political art was largely sidelined.

But I was still looking for a way to merge creation, social change, and dialogue.

Soon, I discovered the architect Christopher Alexander, who had pioneered a method that allowed communities, towns, and neighbors to design their homes and civic buildings alongside him. Today we would call it co-design. At its essence, it was a way of having a collective conversation, and using that conversation to design solutions for that community.

To me, it seemed like an evolution of the work I had been doing, but one that moved from creative political dialogue to a collective creative act. In 1997 I went to grad school for architecture at UC Berkeley to learn more about his practice.

What I soon discovered was the architectural practice of the time was more about individual expression than it was about community engagement. I practiced as an architect at a firm for a short while, but I missed feeling like I was making change, I missed the idea that creativity inspired conversation, things that I had found core to my own creative practice.

Like a lot of people, I had heard about IDEO through watching the iconic shopping cart video on *Nightline*. If you haven't seen it, it follows the process of a large collaborative design team as they take a week to completely redesign a standard shopping cart. We see echoes of the work that team did in redesigned shopping carts everywhere today. To be honest, as I watched, my first thought was, *Wait, someone designs shopping carts?* I thought they just appeared wholly formed in the world. But the essential humanity in the process spoke to my heart. IDEO felt like a place where design and real change could happen.

I joined IDEO in 2000 and built IDEO's architecture practice. The nature of design culture at IDEO was deeply collaborative, and it wasn't hard to extend that collaborative process to include the people we were designing for.

I was personally committed to breaking down the language of architecture to make the process and principles more straightforward, so that our clients could truly be co-designers. We had nurses design patients' rooms. We built rough classroom concepts in full scale and walked and talked through the space with teachers, changing them on the fly. It was design as a constructed and constructive conversation, an evolution of what I'd seen in Alexander's design process.

But while we were doing this work, something very interesting was happening.

Schools, nonprofits, philanthropies, and governments began coming to us to see how we might solve larger, more systemic problems. These were nascent challenges, but I realized that this was the kind of work I really wanted to do. And, not surprisingly, I found myself right back where I started, doing essentially the same thing I'd been doing in college and after: bringing people together to use creativity to make change. And just as with those projects for ACT UP or the Border Arts Workshop, everything we did started with the right conversation.

This was so influential on me, as we began to build a business focused on work with these highly varied organizations coming together to tackle more large-scale, systemic, societal issues like income inequity, gun violence, and health care.

These kinds of projects meant bringing groups together in "tri-sectoral" conversations—nonprofits and foundations, for-profits and private companies, and the government. Those conversations were, of course, incredibly fraught. The three sectors often had wildly divergent reasons for engaging. With that came the subtler issues. Sometimes there was no common language; other times there were different ideas of how a conversation should happen, or even how fast things should move. Very early on in this work, I discovered that when we brought together diverse stakeholders, communities, and political and cultural entities in hopes of making change, our existing tools weren't quite good enough.

A huge turning point for me happened in early 2010. I was in Greece, and I had just spoken out of turn at a gathering of state officials and big money. As I left the room, I was surrounded by a cadre of black suits who prodded me into a back corner. For a brief but very anxious moment I stood penned in place. Suddenly, Greek Prime Minister George Papandreou emerged into the cluster of security. Rather than angry words and banishment, he asked if I would join him for dinner.

Later that night, I found myself sitting in an empty taverna on the Athenian shore with only the prime minister, his special agents, and his wife, Ada, the glamorous first lady of the Mediterranean. His cell phone was ringing nonstop; it was Hosni Mubarak, the former president of Egypt, looking for refuge. We were, after all, in the middle of the Arab Spring. The prime minister looked down at the phone on the table and said,

"Sometime, if we could just slow government down, we could avoid crisis."

At the time it felt strange, maybe even naïve. But in retrospect, I've come to realize that purposely designing slower dialogue may actually allow us to solve big problems. It's simple, but not basic. And it was the first, but by no means the last, time I would gain startling insight on dialogue from the prime minister, a man with original Athenian democracy embedded in his genes. Over the next couple of years, as Greece hurtled toward an economic crisis, and in the subsequent years that it took to process what had happened, George and I had a lot of dialogues about dialogues.

George was very thoughtful and sophisticated about how to step outside any exchange and see the context that was hindering or could improve an interaction. Two world leaders might be deadlocked across a table, he told me, but if we stood side by side in the sea, up to our waists, looking out over the distant horizon, we might find a different kind of accord. He dreamed of a program that would empower Athenian taxi drivers to help incite civic dialogue. No joke. "They are the true moderators of the dialogue" in the street, he told me.

My conversations about conversations with George made something very clear to me: to redesign our social structures, we would in turn have to redesign its core working tool—the conversation itself.

So, we had to start work in earnest on how we could redesign the conversation. The questions were obvious: How could we accelerate the process of building a common language? How could we get people to openly articulate their varied goals? And if we could get people to agreement, how could you be certain that that agreement led to action? While the questions were obvious, the answers took real design effort.

By 2016, we had successfully used new conversation formats to tackle design problems that ranged from work with the American people and the newly formed Consumer Financial Protection Bureau to work with nonprofits and farmers in the Andes. I structured all new kinds of conversations on health, anxiety, and stress with the surgeon general and explored the way dialogue in the town squares of Greek villages might help relieve the weight of the Greek financial crisis. I led new formats with the elite of the Aspen Institute and with the victims of gun violence in Brooklyn.

These formats ranged in scope and intended impact: some were a series of short dynamic lessons on new ways to think about the art of listening, some were targeted to allow hundreds of people to explore new ideas and hypotheses and build support from a crowd in real time. These formats broke conversational conventions, they had new and stricter rules, they incorporated movement or props, there was both choreography and craft in their construction. All of these new ways to have a conversation will be explored in the chapters to come.

We were making progress. We were making conversation.

What Conversations Matter?

You're reading this for the same reason I've been researching this and writing about it: you want the ability to have greater creative impact on the conversations you have and, maybe even more important, you want to have greater creative impact *with* the conversations you have. You know this can happen but first . . . What are the conversations that matter most? How do we recognize conversations that really require and can benefit from a creative approach?

Just because we're talking doesn't mean we're making conversation. Quick chats, catching up over coffee, hallway gossip, late-night laughs with loved ones: these kind of wandering and open interactions can be the best gifts of life. They're so vital for our connection to one another; we long for them when we're alone and apart; besides which, they're fun. But these are not the kinds of conversations we'll be focusing on.

The conversations that matter, the ones we want to center on, are a more substantive and intentional form of engagement. When I think about the conversations that matter, there are typically three things they have in common.

First, there is difference. For many of our hardest conversations to make change, there needs to be difference in the room. The people there can't be all alike or in agreement.

Be careful, though, about what you consider difference to be. Sometimes it's obvious: it will look like a different generation, a different gender, race, or ethnicity.

But often it will be the people who appear similar that end up having very different perspectives and agendas, and the most disruptive points of difference can be disguised. I've been in powerful rooms of all white, affluent European men and women where the difference in politics feels insurmountable. Likewise, I've been in the dining room of a self-described ideal family, where the family dinner, every family dinner, becomes a battleground.

Second, it feels difficult. You can gather all kinds of people in a room and have a discussion about what movie they want to see, but that's not what this kind of conversation is about. If it feels like it's simple and easy, then it's probably not the conversation that needs to be designed. Conversations that matter are about grappling with hard issues. These conversations will often be about strategy, political issues, or emotionally charged topics.

Third, something is made, besides conversation. Too often, we experience a kind of "conversation fatigue," which emerges from the fact that so little seems to come of it. More often than not I hear things like: "We had a great conversation, there was so much agreement and good ideas but then nothing happened." This is the greatest risk: that little comes of it. A creative conversation must *move us forward*. It must help us shift from thinking and talking into the act of doing. Agreement cannot be enough; action is required.

So the purposeful burden that I place on the term *conversation* is that it must work to resolve differences, must explore hard issues, and must be aimed toward a positive outcome.

We're also going to talk a lot in this book about what conversations matter—not broadly in the world, but to you the reader.

Those conversations will vary person to person. There are CEOs of Fortune 500 companies who have complete control of the conversations they have in their boardroom but who will completely collapse in a parent-teacher conversation. Likewise, there are some teachers who purposefully design their conversations to make sure that that same CEO cannot dominate them.

The conversations you decide to exert creative energy on can be global in nature, discussions traversing the dividing lines of international conflict, or the future of climate change. These conversations can also be more personal in nature, exposing hard truths to the ones you love. These seemingly small domestic conversations can be designed too.

When Conversations Go Bad

We all know that feeling when a conversation is starting to founder. Three of the most common symptoms include:

1. There's an evident imbalance in the power dynamics. These may be explicit based on hierarchy or inequality among the people in the room, or implicit where the expertise of a few individuals far exceeds that of the collective. It can be evidenced by a few overpowering voices or the silence of others.

2. There's a lack of certainty about purpose. Gathering people to discuss a topic is not the same as making sure people understand what the goals are for that gathering. Without purpose there's no way to guide a conversation forward. Some may be trying to solve while some are trying to explore, and neither may be the right stance for the conversation.

3. There's a collapse into critique. Often this arises from the conditions listed above where a small subset of participants in a conversation turn from the topic of the conversation to the critique of the conversation

itself. It's the most common and most dispiriting end of a conversation, invalidating it altogether. It's also unfortunately increasingly common.

It's unlikely that any of these will feel unfamiliar and there will be multiple examples of conversations that founder or fall into a downward spiral due to these "symptoms."

When we think of those who can make hard conversations happen, we tend to think of professionals with sophisticated, even extreme, tools: facilitators, mediators, psychologists, hostage negotiators. But . . . approaching dialogue as a designer means that you treat dialogue as something that you create, something that you design, not something that you facilitate. It's tremendously liberating. There are new possibilities, if you can begin to think about how you influence the structure and feel of a conversation by design rather than by pure force of will. It relies not on your interpersonal skills but a different skill set: the ability to spot opportunity and design for it in order to shape outcome and impact.

More important, for many of us these tools allow us to assert creative control over a conversation. Think of creativity as a benevolent power you can exert when conversations start to go astray. The most powerful thing about applying creative constructs to the conversations that you make is that they can help balance power, protect from inequities, and do it in a way that's built into the very structures that govern the conversations. We'll look at formats for conversation where shy people can express themselves, people can test ideas they're unsure of, and critique can feel constructive, even fun and funny. Making conversations helps us make conversations that feel more equitable without requiring us to police the language or the room.

Making Conversation

As I started researching this book, I found hope again. I felt like I could write and speak with optimism about the future of conversation without it being foolish optimism. Why?

Again and again I found evidence of people who had persevered and were making hard conversations happen in all kinds of surprising contexts. I saw more people bridging divides than falling into them. I witnessed people tackling hard topics, not with trepidation but with a kind of excitement, even joy.

I looked at successful spiritual practices. I went on a pilgrimage in Spain and journeyed to the Himalayas to get a sense of why so many people make lifetime bonds with fellow pilgrims. I sat in silence in Quaker meetings to better understand the Quaker mode of listening, witnessing, and testifying, and spoke to rabbis about Passover seders and sitting shiva, both of which created rituals around getting through crisis and using old formats to discuss contemporary issues.

I spoke to psychologists and anthropologists. Some of the conversations with psychologists were about how people use specific tools like silence, or how posture can affect the way you might think and feel about something. But we also talked about the creative process and what we could learn from the psychology of creativity that could apply to the art of conversation. Some of the talks were to help me through just how hard it is to write a book.

And then I turned to artists. I spoke to directors on how theater engages and reengages its audiences. An accomplished playwright talked with me about the creative struggle and how in order to create you couldn't give up and had to continually reevaluate what you had, trying to make something from what can feel like fragments and figments. That certainly is the struggle in hoping for change from dialogue: Will it slip away? Can a group find meaning? Can you make something change or build something new just starting with words?

I sang in choirs that were reinventing protest music and met with Indigenous American storytellers to hear how they incorporated singing into their work. I met with game designers to get a sense of the way rules can change and the nuanced landscape between play and conversation.

Lastly, I looked back over my own lifetime of work as an artist, architect, and designer, searching for the lessons embedded in those experiences.

This book is a compilation of learnings from case after case of people who have made conversation happen. It's a compilation of tips and tricks on ways to navigate the discussions that seem to be failing, and it's packed with practices—some simple, some sophisticated—about how you can begin to get playful and creative with the way a conversation gets made.

It became evident that there are seven essential components, what I think of as the Seven Cs of a creative conversation: Commitment, Creative Listening, Clarity, Context, Constraints, Change, and, ultimately, Creation. Let's look at each of these quickly.

COMMITMENT: Most of us go into conversations with only one goal: convincing everyone else we're right and they're wrong. And why shouldn't we? Sticking to our beliefs makes us feel safe and powerful. But creative conversations are very different. They're about open-ended exploration. Letting go of our own ideas, or at least not holding on to them so tightly. Committing to the conversation itself. Committing to the people we're in conversation with. It's always an act of courage and optimism, and it's just about the hardest thing in the world. So, ask yourself: Am I committed?

CREATIVE LISTENING: Most people aren't good listeners and few of us actually enjoy it. We treat it like a chore, nodding along, keeping dutifully silent, waiting for our turn to talk. Truly, listening can be a creative act—generative, satisfying, and pleasurable. With creative listening, we can learn to help people tell us better stories; to test perspectives other than our own; to embrace our own reactions and judgment. When we listen in this way, we are actively searching for the clues for creation.

CLARITY: Conversations rely on their most basic element: words. But words are fraught with misunderstanding. There is complex or technical jargon not everyone understands. There are words we use every day that we believe have shared meaning but do not. As a result, so many conversations get lost in the gap between the words we hear and the meaning behind the words someone else is using. But if we begin a conversation by seeking clarity and definition of the words and terms we use, we can build a common language and even uncover common values. The right words unite us and show us our way forward together.

CONTEXT: Where you have a conversation has a huge influence on how the conversation goes. The space, literally, sets the script: some rooms give conversations extra energy and life, some turn dialogue inert. We'll learn how to choose the spaces for the conversations you want to have. Sometimes this means re-arranging an available space or moving to another. Sometimes just a subtle shift in position can have a huge impact on the kinds of conversations that are possible.

CONSTRAINTS: Every conversation has rules. But too often the rules are unstated, arbitrary, or unfair. As a result, everyone gets frustrated, nothing feels equitable or productive, and the loud-est voice ends up dominating, reducing the dialogue to their own monologue. But constraints, as any designer will tell you, can fuel creativity. Rules can set us free. First, we have to reject someone else's rule book and start designing better constraints for the conversations we want to have and the communities we want to build. This chapter will explore how we can play with rule sets and constraints to make our dialogues more honest, more fun, safer, and more meaningful.

CHANGE: All creative conversations require a moment of change— when a group of individuals becomes a community intent on creation. This moment of collective change is what allows us to imagine moving a conversation forward and inspires the po-tential for action. The best tools for this can actually be found in some of our oldest and most sacred practices. Familiar and sacred texts, vows and promises that allow us to forge community and authentic connection have always been central to the human experience. They can provide rhythm and thoughtful interruption; they can offer intuitive—if not obvious—paths forward.

CREATION: When do we stop talking and just start doing? So many impactful conversations yield remarkable ideas and so many of those ideas never leave that room. Creation is about moving from actionable ideas to just plain action. Creation means getting real about whether the people in the conversation are the ones who can make the ideas real. Creation is about finding the courage to recommit. Creation is about taking that conversation out into the world.

The seven chapters are sets of tools, but they are also seven steps. They happen in order because they're progressively more difficult. The early work is not easy, but you can do many of the practices on your own. Learning to listen in new ways, for instance, is something you can start trying immediately.

As we progress, the work requires greater engagement from a group. You can set rules on your own, but it takes a group to agree to those rules to make them work. Additionally, work from later in the book often relies on learnings from the earlier ones: it's hard to be good at rule-setting, for example, without making sure you have clarity about the why in the rules.

Additionally, throughout the book there are short "conversation breaks." These sections function much like they would in any large meeting, convening, or long conversation. You know how sometimes you take a break from those kinds of gatherings, and all you want to do is just get something done, send an email, get to the restroom, or grab a snack. But sometimes you find yourself absorbed by someone interesting, and you keep chatting and find yourself getting inspired.

That's the same here. Sometimes the breaks are just quick things you can start doing right now, sometimes they're slightly longer, but they allow you to explore things that might inspire a new approach or new mindset around conversations. Just like in the real world, they're not all the same, but they do give you a moment of action, inspiration, and sometimes just pause.

But mostly I want this book to give you the hope I found.

So, when you feel like you cannot make conversation or when the world seems to be broadcasting that idea, this book should be a reminder that *you can*, and *people are*. Do not succumb.

When a conversation seems hard, when it makes you nervous, when you feel at risk or on edge, remember this core lesson: Conversation is always an act of creativity. We don't have to just be participants in, or victims of, conversations. We can be the makers of the conversations that matter most.

CHAPTER 1

COMMITMENT

> Boundaries must be crossed. First, ideas
> about change must engage people of various
> backgrounds who do not agree about everything.
> Second, people must find themselves in
> places that are not their homes, and among
> groups who were not previously their friends.
>
> —*Timothy Snyder*

Are you committed?"

I'm really asking you, the reader. This is the true start of the book, and I'd like to be sure we're on the same page.

"Are you committed?" It's a question I've been asking people all my life: clients, friends, large groups, my husband. People tend to quickly answer, *Yes, of course. We're committed to our ideas,* they say, *to furthering our goals, conveying our beliefs, advancing our agenda.*

But that's not what I mean at all. In fact, that's the opposite of what I mean.

I'm asking: *Are you committed to having this conversation? Are you committed to the people you're making conversation with?*

That's a very different kind of commitment. And that's our first step: how to commit to a conversation.

Commit to Conversations First, Beliefs Second

My friend and mentor Mary Gentile speaks often on the topic of when and how to "stand up and speak your mind." Once, when she was giving a talk, she took a question from someone in the audience who'd had their hand practically raised from the very beginning of her lecture.

"I always take a stand, I always speak my mind," this person asked, "but nobody ever listens. Why?"

"There's your answer," Mary responded. "Maybe it's about *how* you take a stand."

I heard a variation on this recently from Richard Besser, the CEO of the Robert Wood Johnson Foundation: "It's hard now to have conversations when we hold our beliefs so tight that we no longer just say 'I disagree' but say instead 'I disagree and you're wrong' or worse 'I disagree, you're wrong, and I hate you.'" His words stuck. You can probably take it a step farther. Nowadays we tell people we disagree with: "You're wrong, and I hate you, and you're lying."

It's so easy to blame politics or social media—and, of course, they've amplified disagreements and divisions. But the truth is that this problem begins with one of the most basic and valuable lessons of childhood. From an early age, we're taught to commit to beliefs, to stand up for our values. That's what most people think of initially when I use the word *commitment*.

It makes sense, of course. Formulating beliefs, in the first place, takes work—a lot of work. We're not born with our beliefs in place, though we may in fact inherit them. Developing beliefs takes exploration of ideas and worldviews; it takes discussion with people we trust. We will gradually build evidence for our beliefs and seek out like-minded people who share those beliefs. Eventually we will start to filter our world through the lens of these beliefs. Naturally, we want to commit to them!

Many times, however, our beliefs are literally bred into us, and along with those beliefs there can be biases, intolerance, even hate. Which means that when we are making conversation, we must be willing to evaluate those beliefs and decide whether they will accompany us into our conversations. Truth be told, the beliefs we start with may actually keep us from entering a conversation at all. Beliefs about race, gender, and class difference in general can stop us from ever making conversation in the first place.

As we explore the idea of conversation as a creative act, we will need to redefine the things we commit to. We need to be less a defender of our beliefs, and instead commit to the process by which we manufacture beliefs: exploration, community, and conversation.

Numerous psychological studies of childhood development suggest the value of community in helping children form beliefs. In essence we are returning to that earlier mode of belief exploration and formation.

The knowledge that maybe children knew something we well-meaning adults had forgotten was exactly why I traveled to the John Dewey Academy in Great Barrington, Massachusetts.

The first thought that popped into my mind as I drove through the giant stone gates was, *It's Hogwarts*. It's a castle, really, anchored in place by four oversized turrets almost as wide as they are tall, the entry is bracketed by a great stone archway, and you enter through massive wooden doors, the handles of which need two hands to turn. Though the day was hot, entering the dark main hall was like entering into the cool of a cave. True to the Hogwarts analogy, the great hall seemed larger on the inside than it did from outside. Ornate wooden staircases zigzagged several stories up, Escher-like.

The students who choose to attend John Dewey Academy— and they do choose—are choosing to attend a school that is in session all year round. Many may not see or speak to their parents for months at a time; they will be entirely drug free (doctor-prescribed meds included); and they will be responsible for all maintenance, cleaning, and cooking in the castle.

They are in a sense lost children, most of them are there because they have "flamed out" or "self-imploded," teenagers suffering from serious addictions—though it is interesting to note that the form of addiction has shifted radically over the years. When the John Dewey Academy began, drugs, alcohol, and violent behavior were the core of the student pathologies. Today, some teens there still struggle with chemical addictions, but there are just as many addicted to gaming, social media, porn; they don't act out but rather fall inward. Many are unable to communicate in social situations, preferring email and text to speaking aloud. As a teacher who's taught math at Dewey for eighteen years told me, "It was almost easier when they were confrontational."

They're also a pretty diverse group. I met students from the upper echelons of Manhattan high society, from the rural south and Midwest, and from abroad as far as China and India. There is no reason to believe these children could coexist much less become caregivers to each other over the course of the years they spend at school.

The headmaster, Andrea Lein, PhD in clinical and school psychology, believes Dewey works because it is a "safe space." In our present culture the term *safe space* is used with many different intentions. Sometimes it can describe environments where people can be certain that they will not hear or need to engage with ideas offensive to them. Tension over this concept has popped up, particularly on college campuses. Some students choose to be sheltered from values that are not their own and from conversations that may offend, which, others argue, is one of the foundational values of higher education and the liberal arts.

Dewey is not that kind of safe space. Andrea clarifies, "The concept of safe space here is very different from how most people are using it. I do think that this is a safe space and we want to create a safe space, but safe space in the sense that we can all have enough trust with one another to be honest— radically honest at times—and share truths in such a way that we can learn to respect differences. We don't want to have to walk on eggshells. *We really don't want to walk on eggshells here.*"

Dewey works, and the conversations they have do cure these

children, but it all happens because of commitment. This is a collection of children who, for various reasons, have lost their ability to participate in day-to-day society, yet here conversation is the foundation of their "cure." As one mother described it to me, once you join, you are all "committed to a relentless and ongoing conversation about how they will progress."

That commitment allows for something magical to happen—as befits a fairy-tale castle. Dewey, as Andrea defines it, is a safe space because all ideas—hard ideas, controversial ideas, potentially offensive ideas—can be discussed, and there is a commitment to the safety of the community and the values that support open and honest dialogue. *Dewey is a refuge for those conversations.* Everything that happens at Dewey happens through a process of open and involved conversations: setting rules, the consequences for breaking rules, their own progress and education—all of it is an ongoing conversation.

The Dewey school is an extreme but inspiring example of commitment. A creative conversation is about *choosing to hold your existing beliefs more lightly*; it's about committing to exploration and to staying engaged with a set of people that will help you in that exploration. In essence this means that the same process that allowed you to build the belief and value set you have now is the exact same process that will allow you to explore new beliefs and establish new communities.

This is so simple and yet it is an unbelievably difficult shift in mindset. You will be, in many ways, going against the grain of contemporary patterns in dialogue, but that's a good thing. Start slowly, practice with friends and family—people you already feel committed to, which will, by the way, reveal just how hard it can be to make this shift. At the same time, however, it might help you feel firsthand the power a commitment to exploration and open-mindedness can have.

Open the Door to Difference

At IDEO, we did a lot of work with WW (Weight Watchers). Their meetings are perfectly engineered for length and content, but people get up to the door and won't go in. It's a huge hurdle, and the leaders just couldn't see it. So one morning I took their CEO and a group of executives to an African American megachurch in Dallas.

As soon as they saw the backup on the highway—that's how popular this place was, drawing thirty thousand parishioners every Sunday—they started to grow uneasy and wanted to beg off. Their discomfort only grew as we were waved into the Disneyland-size parking lot, approaching a church so vast it looked like a Costco, and merged into the crowd, all black, all in their Sunday best. This is Dallas: The hair was *real*. "We're going to stand out," they were saying. "We should turn back."

They were experiencing the exact same moment of hesitation as every would-be WW member. Before a meeting you notice people lingering, scoping out the room, checking out the attendees. They will do it discreetly, passing by the door to the room once or twice, glancing quickly inside. They will do it from afar, sitting in their parked car outside the WW branch, keeping an eye out for those who enter. They are checking out who's entering and seeking difference.

Am I bigger? Am I smaller? Am I the only man? It's routine to ask themselves: *Are these people like me? Am I going to stand out? Am I going to offend or feel uncomfortable?* When they see too much difference, people opt out of meetings at that moment, and that's when the excuse comes in. They tell themselves, "I just don't have the time."

It's second nature to scan, assess, and look for difference— pretty much anytime we find ourselves in a group. We do it as we walk into a room, when we scan email invites to a meeting, when we look at paperless-post RSVP lists to a party or read the bios for a conference. We do this because it's easy to believe that *the more different* the people in the conversation, *the more difficult* it will be.

But here's the thing: once you go through that door, once you attend your first meeting and sit with people bigger than you, smaller than you, in essence different from you, you realize that that difference does not stop the meeting from being supportive and helpful.

(The WW executives, by the way, found the courage to go into the church. Not only did the meeting provide inspiration for what could happen at scale—thirty thousand people is more like a concert than a church service—but they found that the people they sat with were kind, loving, and not at all different from people they knew who attended their own meetings.)

Very simply, open the door to difference.

There's a scene I love in the Hal Ashby film *Harold and Maude* where the shy and reserved Harold turns to Maude after watching her engage with strangers at an amusement park and asks her how it is that she's so good with people. She gestures in a matter-of-fact way and says, "Well, they're my species."

That idea is worth keeping in mind.

As a *species* we are more similar than not. Across our species we are weakened by disease, across our species we are hurt by violence and chaos, across our species we thrive in conditions of prosperity and plenty. I've spent my career working across class and cultural boundaries and making conversations with the affluent as well as the impoverished. I've worked on health care at Mayo Clinic and with field doctors in rural India, or creating financial services for the extraordinarily wealthy and for those living on the very edge of poverty. I've observed spouses hide money in a shoebox to safeguard it from their husbands; I've observed others who hide it in an account on the Cayman Islands. In the end they're still hiding money from someone. While the conditions and cultural context are different, many of the aspirations, goals, things that give pride remain the same—so it is with the things that cause us fear and anxiety. Furthermore, across cultures, the way we celebrate, mourn, worship, or wed are at their essence more similar than they are different.

That does not mean we're not different—we of course are—but we are still the same species.

Ask for the Conversation You Want

The first day that my husband and I moved to New York, I was alone in our apartment when the movers arrived. They spent the better part of the day hauling our furniture up multiple flights of steps; the apartment was hot and disorderly, and the movers clearly exhausted. As the furniture stacked up in the middle of the apartment, I stood alone in a brand-new city completely overwhelmed, feeling like I was about to burst into tears.

As I stood there totally lost and uncertain, there was a loud knock at the door. I opened it to see the angry face of the woman who lived in the apartment below ours. She was furious. "Do you know anything about the building rules?" she yelled. I'd violated all of them. I'd blocked her stairwell for part of the day . . . the noise of the move was outrageous and so on.

I was already feeling anxious and that anxiety began to bloom into an uncontrollable anger. Here was the proverbial in-your-face New Yorker, and she was our neighbor no less, and I was not going to be some wuss from California. I'd give back as hard as she gave. All of that and more rushed through my mind, but somehow before I just let her have it, I found myself asking a very straightforward question—I'm sure with a bit of tremor in my voice.

"Is this really the way we want to start our conversation?" I was utterly surprised, and she seemed even more so. She stopped, looked at me for a moment or two, and made a decision.

"No," she said, "it isn't."

We restarted the conversation, speaking in a different tone. I offered apologies, she offered help. We ended up living in that apartment for three years and became close friends with this downstairs neighbor. Months later, when Hurricane Sandy hit and we were all struck by the blackout, she joined us in our apartment with a lot of candles and a few bottles of wine to make it through the unsettling night.

Think about it. How many conversations have you had—conversations that matter, with people that matter—that you *know* could have had a different tone? A different feeling? And yet we let them go wrong, despite our instincts. Often the tone of a conversation is an unconscious reaction to a situation, or to the first few moments of the interaction. And then we find ourselves trapped, with the conversation unfolding around us, determined by what we feel in that moment rather than what we want or need to accomplish.

Why would anyone commit to a conversation that they don't want, has the wrong tone, or has already got off on the wrong foot?

So I just think about that moment with my neighbor, and the lesson that's stuck with me since: *try asking for the conversation you want.*

Pick the Conversations You Want to Commit To

Thinking of every conversation as one that you need to design would get fairly exhausting fairly quickly, and it would remove the pleasure that we associate with conversation and dialogue. Choosing to commit to a conversation means getting good at assessing what matters most to you. Whether it's a personal or a professional situation, what do you want to *make* of the conversation?

You might be the CEO of a company and yet, today, the most crucial conversation might be a parent-teacher conference. You might be a political activist who feels confident in a crowd but grows uncomfortable with family around a holiday dinner table. That's why it's useful to roughly break down the kinds of conversations that matter into three categories. The first two are fairly practical and generalizable; the third is more specific to you and will rely on your own intuition.

CONVERSATIONS WITH A GOAL: These may be the easiest to spot. These are conversations that are meant to solve a problem or speculate on a future vision. These can be individual: What are my career goals? They can be broader and institutional: How does our organization have impact or how do we solve a big problem? They can be societal: How can this coalition reduce homelessness or what can this city do to stop gun-related deaths?

These kinds of conversations often fall into the category of strategy setting. Establishing a strategy—in all industries, settings, and sectors—is a form of conversation. Sometimes it's an extended conversation, if you are setting a long-term strategy, or sometimes more succinct, if you are establishing a strategy for a discrete issue. I've based my life's work on the idea that all strategy conversations should be treated with some form of creativity. In part because I believe it leads to better solutions, but also because setting a strategy for impact in the world should feel exhilarating and exciting. Good conversations about strategy really need a commitment from all to actively engage in exploration, wandering, and divergence, but because you are looking to establish a plan, that exploration needs to be guided. This is where this book will come into play.

CONVERSATIONS TO BUILD AGREEMENT OR UNDERSTANDING: If strategy conversations are about commitment to exploration, conversations to build agreement offer a chance to realign and recommit the community to established goals. At home and in your personal life, these can be the kinds of things referred to as "family meetings," which often happen in response to a moment when it feels like there is a lack of alignment of expectations or a violation of "the rules." At work, this may entail extending the work of a smaller strategy team to the entire organization. (It may also be a variant on the family meeting: a conversation that is meant to course-correct work cultures or maybe even establish that work culture in the first place.)

CONVERSATIONS THAT SCARE YOU: This last category is something only you can assess, but in many ways it's the most crucial category. I exaggerate slightly when I use the word "scare," but the intent is to point out that the feelings you'll have when you think about these conversations will be akin to what you feel when you are afraid. It might be something that sets your skin tingling, or makes your stomach feel butterflies—not in the good way. It suggests a conversation that you feel is somehow unsafe. Perhaps it's about the people in the conversation: Do they hold power over you or make you feel intimidated? Might you discover something unpleasant or cause conflict?

These are often the conversations we most need to make happen. They will make you stronger and they frequently deepen your connections to the people you care most about.

When *Not* to Commit

Despite everything, if you cannot find it in yourself to commit to a conversation, then . . . don't.

Not only can it be the right thing for you, it is always the right thing to do for the benefit of a productive conversation. In my experience, a huge percentage of conversations that fail do so when one or more people in that conversation aren't really committed to it but aren't honest with themselves or others about why they can't or won't commit.

We've probably all had the experience of being annoyed with the naysayer in the room when we're trying something new—and most of us have also had the experience of *being* the naysayer or doubter. No matter which side of the conversation you're on, lack of commitment can kill creativity and progress, not to mention cultivate a tone of frustration and ambivalence in the community.

I encourage you to reflect on the conversations that matter and be rigorous with yourself. Is it your intention to aim for a common goal? Can you commit to the people you're in the room with?

But sometimes making a commitment to conversation is really too much—when you don't sense the other parties take the work seriously, when there doesn't seem to be a plan, when the tone doesn't feel honest, supportive, and safe.

Choosing *not* to commit takes self-awareness but it also takes discipline. However, it can be a gift to yourself and the conversation when you realize things can happen without your being a part of it.

Making Conversation: Committing to Principles

When I worked with Mayo Clinic, I was deeply inspired by how uniquely sensitive the staff were to their patients, how uniformly dedicated and service-minded their people were, no matter their role, be they the doctors, receptionists, nurses, or custodial staff. If you visit Mayo Clinic, you'll see evidence everywhere of two principles in particular: "sympathy and empathy with patients and family," and to "inspire hope."

Once, I attended their orientation for new employees. The history of the institution, the commitment to science, and the story of the Mayo brothers were all explored in depth. What was interesting to note about orientation was that it was attended by all new employees *whether you were going to be mopping the floors or were a top surgeon in your field*. Everyone was taught the principles and mission of the organization at the same time. It's that commitment to founding principles that makes Mayo's culture so unique.

Just as any good work culture—or for that matter any good community culture—has principles, good conversations should have principles as well. Principles are a plan for what you will commit to.

When I moved to the New York office of IDEO, one of the first things we built was a series of quarterly public talks with 92nd Street Y called *Break and Make*. The format was simple—a conversation between two CEOs in the same industry. One would be at the top of the industry, an organization on the rise; the other would be a heritage company, well known in the world but not necessarily known for new and innovative things. For example, we brought together David Kirchhoff, then CEO of Weight Watchers, with co-CEOs of SoulCycle Julie Rice and Elizabeth Cutler to give each other advice on leading fast-growing companies. It was a generous, warm, and honest conversation.

Early on, we received two pieces of feedback through the comment cards we distributed to the audience that I couldn't get out of mind. One was: "You're such creative people, I don't understand why you would use a panel format." The other: "It was such an interesting conversation; I wish that there was a way for more of the audience to participate." It seemed *Break and Make* was broken from the beginning.

A few of us gathered and decided that, before we did any more events, we needed something to allow us to tune these public conversations, something that not only set the tone but also gave us a set of guidelines as we designed conversations.

We needed principles.

So we looked at what we liked about *Break and Make*— for instance, the organizations involved were grappling with significant disruption, but the conversation was in no way sensationalist. It was low-key and people felt fairly comfortable talking about the issues they were struggling with. We liked that tone and wanted to keep it.

Our first principle was: Our creative conversations should feel "humble and honest."

Also core to *Break and Make* was that the people onstage were asked to help each other. So we built out the second principle: Our conversations should be "generous and helpful." If you joined, you might find someone else in the conversation who could be of help or vice versa.

But we'd heard critiques too. The event didn't feel inclusive enough. People wanted to participate—they had enough of just watching conversations happen. We decided on the "democratic" principle both to give the feel of who we wanted in the room and the feel for the way the conversation happened. We thought elite talking to elite was pretty dull, and the people who came together wanted a chance to engage with each other.

Those principles became the basis of six years of creative conversations.

The primary goal of the principles is to inform the tone, feel, and intention of the conversation. Is it about team building? Then you may choose three principles, such as light, open-ended, and interactive. Maybe it's about informing employees of a new HR policy, so you may choose three principles, such as serious, helpful, but still interactive.

Generating a set of principles for a conversation can help you commit to and ultimately design conversations, but simply listing them won't make them magically appear in a conversation. They are aspirations for the conversation, and the creative work we explore in this book will help you make your conversations bring those principles to life.

Courage and Conversation

With commitment comes courage.

When I speak to students, work with clients, and often in moments of hopelessness with design teams, I always remind them that there are moments when they must choose to be brave; there is no other way forward. It may not be climbing Mount Everest, but it's a kind of "everyday bravery" that we need more of when we design conversations. Commitment requires courage, and you actually need to practice courage. The more you practice, the more confident you will be in the conversations you commit to.

After the death of my brother—a chef with a chef's propensity for late-night tattoos—I chose to get a tattoo as a way to keep him close: I wanted the single word *brave* above my heart, where I would see it daily. I did this to remind myself that it takes bravery to navigate even daily life. Seeing it every morning in the mirror is a reminder that I will inevitably be faced with a moment where courage is required and that I should not forget to try to be brave. Courage doesn't just happen; it needs to be taught and, moreover, it *needs to be practiced.* You don't just have courage; it is something that you need to work at, take small steps toward.

While the rest of the world is telling you that making conversation is hard, that it's happening less and less, and that we are only seeing greater and greater divide and difference, *that is not what I experienced when I was researching for this book.* People are having hard conversations. They are committing to other people and opening the door to difference. And one of the things that's helping them do that brave and committed act is thinking about conversations creatively.

The rest of the book is designed not only to help you practice courage but to inspire courage. Creativity in a conversation allows you to fundamentally rethink the way you make conversations. It gives you new tools, new sources of inspiration, and allows for a new way forward. In this case, I'm not suggesting that you need courage to be creative but rather that creativity will give you courage.

So here we go: *Are you committed?*

Conversation Break: The Conversation Notebook

Grace Coddington, the creative director at large for *Vogue*, once said, "Always keep your eyes open. Keep watching. Because whatever you see can inspire you." It's a quote I steal frequently when I teach. The world deserves your attention.

That's why I encourage all creative people, all design teams, and anyone embarking on a creative exploration to keep a notebook. The focus of this kind of work is not processing emotional well-being—it's not a diary. While reading this book I'd like you to consider keeping a "conversation notebook." That journal should have three parts to it.

1. CONVERSATIONS THAT MATTER

This part should focus on the list of conversations that feel the most important to you, the ones you choose to commit to. As discussed in the first part of this chapter, those can be conversations that are important to you professionally; they can be conversations where the people in it feel deeply important to you; and they can and should include a few "challenger" conversations, those where the people in them are quite different from you, conversations that scare you a bit.

2. INSPIRATIONS

When I'm making a conversation, I almost always start by asking participants to share examples of conversations they've been in that triggered the kind of outcome they wanted. Believe it or not, it's hard. So often people remember conversations that went bad or didn't deliver. But they are less aware of the moments that have gone really well, in part because we imagine those conversations were effortless. We need to start being more aware of conversations that go well, and when possible begin to assess what made that happen.

The second part of your notebook should be akin to the way you might keep, say, a travel journal or a journal of other kinds of interesting and inspiring experiences—but focused on the conversations you've been a part of or witnessed that day or that week. Which ones felt good and productive to you? Which ones less so? Who was in that conversation and what was their conversational style? Where was that conversation, what was the context, and what kinds of rules, implicit or explicit, were in action? Keeping eyes—and all senses—open to the conversations around you is about unearthing clues to conversations you like, things you might want to try, and things you aspire to create. Inspiration is the clue to creation.

These things don't have to be extreme or spectacular; instead look at the simple places where good conversations tend to happen. For instance, here's one place I look to for inspiration: breakfast, specifically breakfast out. I love to meet new people for breakfast meetings.

You're sitting down before the stresses of work happen, but typically after morning email has been dispatched. Earlyish morning is also physiologically and chemically the time of the day that we are predisposed to optimism. The meal itself helps set the tone and rhythm: it's cheap and easy, not too many choices, so no anxiety. You catch up on life before ordering, hit the topic at hand while eating, and a promise of sorts is made while paying the bill. Those moments actually allow for a pause, and a chance to reset the base of the conversation. Breakfast places usually have life and activity enough to keep us alert but are still warm and quiet enough to keep you focused on each other.

Usually we're done ten minutes before the hour, no stress about what's next, or worry the conversation would stretch too long. Look around the next time you're at breakfast: good conversations will be happening all around you. Observing the context of conversations can unearth a significant number of clues about what made them so good.

3. YOUR PLANS

When we're getting ready to host a ten-person dinner party, or training for a marathon, or going on an exotic vacation, or starting a big project at work, we make a plan. We'd never just wing it or make it up as we go. That would be ridiculous. But that's because those are complex things we know can be hard, and we plan for hard things.

If we planned conversations better, if we put more creative thinking into them, we could find a resolution without it feeling forced. The right creative practice in a conversation can offer moments of surprise and delight right when we feel most distressed. A well-planned conversation should allow for more difference and more exploration with less anxiety; it should open us up to more authenticity and more ways to get more voices in the room; it can offer more clarity of direction. A plan is a sign for hope.

So what does a plan look like?

A plan in conversation can be pretty simple: an understanding of a goal, a perspective on what potential obstacles might be, and a few tools to help you get past it. The results of planning can be significant, but the components of a plan are familiar.

The final section of this notebook is less about recording past events and more about projecting—think of it like an artist's sketchbook—the conversations you want to create. They can be real existing conversations that are coming up, or ones you might want to design in the future. They should have a name—we'll talk about the why of naming later. A set of principles. An idea of who's in the conversation. And then a description of a plan, and this plan can pull from the tools and points of inspiration embedded in the chapters throughout this book.

CHAPTER 2

CREATIVE LISTENING

Attention is the rarest and purest
form of generosity.

—*Simone Weil*

My mother's only brother was born deaf. So in her childhood home listening was unfairly distributed, and when the silence was broken, it was something special, a gift. Her fluency with sign language gave an extra expressiveness to her gestures and physicality. Even when she was "only" listening, she seemed kinetic, energized by the words being said. She was a magical listener. With just the simplest of questions, she could conjure stories from people who seemed as still as stone. So open, generous, and encouraging that people shared harder, with hope and willingness. They wanted her to know more.

When she was in her early forties—and I was in my midtwenties—she had a massive stroke that left her physically paralyzed and her mind completely remapped. Listening became laborious, a struggle. But there was still beauty in it. When I sat and spoke to her, she would hold the side of my face as though she could pluck the words I said from my mouth and place them directly into her ears.

I can't say that I've always been the best listener. It wasn't for lack of opportunity: I must have one of those faces, because the strangest people at a party and on a street will always just come up to me and start talking. Yet for a long time, I was too self-conscious and annoyed to actually listen to them. Nowadays, I find myself doing too many other things, or simply forgetting to listen at all.

A few years back, I started to notice that these bad listening habits had wormed their way into some of IDEO's design teams. I watched as designers spent more time typing what people were saying, taking dictation, rather than truly listening to what was being said. They lost eye contact, missed gestures and other nuances of expression. At first, I would ask them to "listen like their mother." However, I very quickly learned that people's relationships with their mothers were far too complicated to use as a shorthand recommendation.

So I went back to thinking about my mother—parsing out the qualities of listening she embodied. How she made it seem like an art form, amazing, uplifting, and powerful. From her, I learned that listening is not passive; it is exploration, a way of investigating the world around you, a generative act that helps you discover things about yourself and others simultaneously. So, I knew the feeling generated from good listening.

But what is listening? I wanted to break it down, understand it, make it a learnable skill. This was not just important for our work with clients—it is important for our work with each other and beyond.

You can't even begin to make conversation without establishing new ways to listen. So how do we do it? How do we move from not listening to listening? How do we go from listening out of a sense of duty to listening as a mode of joyful discovery? While I was writing this book, I was determined to experience the landscape of listening—genuine listening. In this chapter, I share some of the lessons I've learned, and hopefully they'll help you too.

Why We're Bad at Listening

When was the last time you raised your hand? Was it in a lecture, a classroom, a meeting? Were you in a crowd or just a small group? Did your hand shoot up high or did you hold it meekly against your chest, hoping not to be noticed?

This habit, ingrained from earliest childhood, is for most of us our first formal lesson in listening. The teacher asks a question, you raise your hand, wait to be called on, then answer. It's orderly, familiar. "You can't very well control the flow of learning and discussion while being interrupted every few minutes," says one teaching manual. Hand-raising is inseparable from our vision of classroom learning—Google "kids in school" and guess what image pops up first? It remains, long after we enter the real world, a sign of engagement and attentiveness.

It's worth looking a little more closely at this practice of hand-raising. How did you really feel, hand up, waiting for your turn? Perhaps you experienced a mild anxiety, or a burst of adrenaline—maybe a twinge of fear. (Beta-blockers, a form of blood pressure medicine, are often taken by people who speak in public to avoid that spike of emotion, which is real and physical.) Yes, there might have been a funny and tingly sort of attentiveness.

Most likely, you felt an intense focus on yourself. Your whole awareness narrowed from the room to you. Raising your hand can be a tremendous act of bravery, but it's not necessarily proof that you're listening. It's a signal that you're waiting. And further, your focus at that point is likely on your awareness that you're waiting.

We're told over and over that being good at anything—being a good partner, a good boss, a good friend—starts with listening. But what no one seems to acknowledge is that listening is hard.

First, as the hand-raising example makes clear, our physiology and anxiety compete with it: trying to listen with intensity can often turn on our fight-or-flight instincts, the blood pumping in our ears, our inner voice drowning out everyone else.

Second, it's difficult to tell if listening is even happening. When others are quiet and generally looking in our direction, we assume that they're listening. But silence is often the faultiest indicator of listening. Quiet is a signal of so much else—boredom, drowsiness, daydreaming, sleep, distraction. This is true from our own experiences: we've all found ourselves sitting across from other people, looking into their eyes, only to realize minutes later we haven't heard a thing they've said. We recognize our poor listening in that moment. But do they?

Third, the way we talk about listening makes it seem like the least compelling and least inspiring of the ways we engage with other people: it is arduous ("We held six listening sessions"), or punitive ("I'm going to give them a good listening-to"), or a command ("Listen up, people"). It's a necessary evil, a task, a chore.

In truth, the whole modern era has been a long and unrelenting attack on listening. Historically, there wasn't much competition for our attention. If you didn't want to listen, you pulled a Thoreau, and ghosted to the quiet of the woods. If we go back just a short while to the middle of the last century, we can find the moment where listening to other people, especially the people around you, started to devolve. It turns out that it's not just that we lost good listening skills, we actually redefined what listening was. We shifted our listening from a form of exploration to a form of consuming. The beginning of this was the introduction of a technology that taught us how *not* to listen: the television.

In the early 1950s we gave the family dinnertime over to the television. In 1952, the first national advertising campaign for the TV tray—a metal or wood table, elaborately decorated or quite plain, with a set of folding legs, easily stacked in a corner, such a deceptively simple concept—was released. One year later, Swanson invented the complementary TV dinner. By 1955 the remote control became a fixture in our homes and what started as avoiding commercials moved us quickly into the realm of channel surfing. Changing channels without getting up was not the big innovation—a device that taught us to divide our attention was. We'd built a system into our lives that built bad listening behaviors into our and our children's lives.

Today, when I do research in people's homes, it's interesting to note the devolution of the dining room. Like an old beloved childhood toy, the dining room table is often neglected or just as often piled with papers, books, mail, or unfolded laundry. Many people use their dining room table as a desk. The dining room, the place used to sit and eat and talk with family and friends about the day's important events, is largely vestigial in American homes today.

Programming innovations happened alongside the rising popularity of television in the home. In 1952 the national political conventions were televised for the first time. A young newsman named Walter Cronkite led the coverage for CBS, and eventually he would become more than just an anchor to the news; he was the anchor to our evenings, maybe even a more present father figure than our own. As it expanded, programming began to compete more aggressively with the attention we paid to each other. In fact, in 1957, the United Kingdom was forced to end the "toddlers' truce," the required dark period of programs between 6:00 and 7:00 p.m., when parents could put their children to bed without missing a television show.

Behaviors that were built during the golden age of television have created patterns of attention and listening that we now consider normal. Children grow up with this forever background noise. Multitasking has become a consciously learned behavior, and entertainment a reward for passive engagement. We fall asleep staring at our screens and fire them up before we're even fully awake again; the result is that disturbing news content is now the first and last thing we see every day. In our research when we ask people where and how they heard the latest headline, they don't even know. The news is there, apparently sourceless and constant. We have willingly chosen divided attention.

Why Active Listening Isn't the Solution

One of the more commonly espoused listening techniques is a practice called "active listening." In spirit it's well meaning but in practice it sucks.

The roots of active listening date back to the 1950s, when Carl Rogers, a psychologist, introduced an idea that seems fundamental now, but was completely novel at the time: person-centered therapy. His thinking was that universal theories of mental health disregarded the fundamental uniqueness of every human being. This new therapeutic practice was instead based around an open-ended, lightly guided set of questions that nudged the patient toward self-analysis.

This idea of listening as a way to help the speaker get what they need to say out there is certainly a service to the speaker, but it deadens the impact and joy for the listener. This form of active listening is commonly taught as a leadership practice and more pervasively is the dominant practice of human resources. Active listening is respectful, appears engaged, and most of all it's safe—but just because you're listening doesn't mean you agree or are even engaged.

A tip from an online forum: "If you're finding it particularly difficult to concentrate on what someone is saying, try repeating their words mentally as they say them—this will reinforce their message and help you stay focused." Ugh.

Another lesson from an important business journal covering the basics of active listening: "Although some positive words of encouragement may be beneficial to the speaker, the listener should use them sparingly so as not to distract from what is being said or place unnecessary emphasis on parts of the message." Really? "Uh-huh" or "go on" are suggested: they encourage people to speak without implying that you agree with them.

Sure, the idea of being open, engaged, and nonjudgmental feels right. But in truth we're right back at that hand-raising moment in class, feigning engagement while actually merely waiting. Indeed, the practices of active listening are so focused on triggering change in the speaker that we lose the fact that listening is an act of learning for the listener.

This new Rogerian therapeutic practice was based on an open-ended, lightly guided set of questions that nudged the patient toward self-analysis while offering only encouragement.

This was such a simple and recursive structure that it actually became a model for one of the earliest language-based computer interfaces. In the mid-1960s, MIT built ELIZA, a computer that spoke with the human participant using a Rogerian technique. (Its name, of course, was taken from the playwright George Bernard Shaw's Eliza Doolittle, the poor cockney woman who learned proper English and manners.) A sample:

I am the psychotherapist. Please, describe your problems. Each time you are finished talking, type RET twice.

I am unhappy.

Are you unhappy often?

Yes.

Can you elaborate on that?

Too much work.

Why do you say too much work?

I am working a lot.

Earlier you said you felt unhappy.

Yes.

I would appreciate it if you would continue.

Well, I don't know what to do.

Maybe your plans have something to do with this.

No, they don't.

Go on, don't be afraid.

I'm depressed.

What causes you to be depressed?

When I was a child, we had a version of ELIZA on our first computer. My friends and I would pass snowy afternoons in downtown Chicago trying to get some kind of emotional rise—any kind of emotional variance—out of our "therapist." Of course, it never actually worked and most often we'd angrily turn off the computer in frustration. ELIZA was an algorithm, a prebuilt script, so of course we couldn't affect its thinking. ELIZA just imitated listening.

The ELIZA example feels like a parody, but it's fairly close to the form of active listening we now hold as a best practice both in the workplace and in the world.

But there is another way of listening. A listening "practice" that allows for joy and discovery, that builds connection between the listener and the person being listened to. There is a way to listen that feels exploratory and, if we let it, it will feel more human, more natural, and more fun. I call it creative listening—by introducing the idea of short, well-told stories, the pleasures of gossip, and sometimes listening less intently, we can introduce incubation and observation, which allows us to make different kinds of conversation.

Let Words Wash Over You

OK, so how do we relearn how to listen? Here's the one way to start: do something else entirely.

Let me explain.

My friend and colleague Beth would be the first to tell you that she once had a listening problem. It wasn't that she didn't listen, but like many of us she listened too fast. She was, or felt like she was, way ahead of the speaker in every conversation.

She would start interrupting declaring, "I know where you're going . . ."

To her credit, she was aware of her "listening problem" and she tried every form of holding back, but even then, she found herself waiting, not speaking but still just waiting for when she would speak next.

And then she took up knitting.

It was a matter of timing. Beth found herself in a full-on baby boom; all of her friends were giving birth to children and she'd made a commitment to knit every newborn a blanket. The sheer number of pregnancies meant that her knitting time started to expand from at home to sitting on planes, and eventually to the workplace. Beth began knitting in meetings and suddenly everything changed.

For others in the meeting it was, at first, a bit unsettling. Knitting was such a "domestic" thing, it felt slightly odd in the business context. But as soon as we got used to balls of wool sitting on meeting tables and the soft clicking of knitting needles—better than the clicking of a keyboard, by the way—the benefits became clear. Beth listened and in truth she was listening in a different way. The slow, methodic nature of her knitting shifted the rhythm of the way she participated; she didn't interrupt, she still added, but when she did, it was calm and thoughtful, almost serene.

What we discovered, what Beth discovered, is the power of a meditative repetitive motion to build a mindful listening practice. In her article "Doodling & Knitting," Nancy Chick calls out that these kinds of mindful tasks are in fact the opposite of multitasking. She cites a study on doodling in which doodlers had almost 30 percent more recall of what had been said than those taking notes. The form of mindful listening that Beth was practicing, knitting in a meeting, kept her attentive to the conversation despite not giving us the traditional cues apparent in "active listening."

This mindful listening is evident throughout history. By happenstance I was recently at a lunch with the artist, designer, and former state historian of New Mexico Estevan Rael-Gálvez. As is the case nowadays, we started talking about talking, specifically about important conversations in Native communities, important decisions, and of course listening.

We were meeting again later, and he promised to bring me some historic artifacts, photos of conversations among local tribal elders, that he thought I'd find intriguing. I'd expected to be shown photographs of formal gatherings, but what he brought surprised me. He showed me two vintage photographs. One was of elder women sitting on an earthen floor husking corn; the other, older men sitting in straight-back chairs on the porch looking out over the village. He explained that in his mind the most significant and thoughtful conversations between village elders often happened over semi-mindless tasks. With partial attention paid to the work at hand, the conversation about key issues in the village were discussed in a slow and thoughtful way. What he described was "mindful listening."

It struck me then that we've always known how to listen in a mindful way, but we've begun to fool ourselves. We've begun to replace mindless actions—like knitting, shucking corn, doodling—with things that feel like they're mindless but actually require concentration. We fool ourselves into thinking that texting, Googling, typing notes on a computer are mindless and still allow us to listen but of course it's the opposite. Perhaps there's a kind of memory of what it means to listen while our hands are busy that has gotten out of line with the devices at hand.

Listening as Incubation

"If God has ever spoken, then God is still speaking, is always speaking."

So begins my introduction to my first Quaker meeting. Inside the Brooklyn Meetinghouse, the old wood-and-upholstery pews have been turned at right angles to each other so that the whole room faces inward. The woman who shook my hand when I entered had referred to the room as a sanctuary, which was enough to almost make me turn around and leave—I didn't want to intrude on anyone's sanctuary. But now that I've settled into the pew and am warmed by the winter sun streaming in through the huge wood window panes, I feel less nervous.

So much of Quaker religion and society rely on true and present engagement. For most of their history, Quakers did not use written contracts. They relied instead on community business meetings to resolve an issue, with the complete group needing to come to an agreement—a kind of testing through listening. Doing that meant patience and attentiveness, elocution and perseverance. Not surprisingly, the Quakers have developed a sophisticated form of listening over the last four hundred years.

As the meeting starts, some people choose to close their eyes; some look about the room or upward. The body language is not of meditation or of prayer. It is attentive. A pretty woman in a red sweater in the corner leans forward, eyes open, chin in her hand, like Rodin's thinker. An attractive gray-haired couple who look like they're probably dancers cock their heads to the side in identical attention, the kind of tilt you'd expect from a curious dog. People are listening to whatever's inside them.

My mind, restless at first, falls into a passive state. I let the silence, the rustles, and the soft coughs pass over me. Gradually my mind moves from thinking about listening to actual listening. In my own work as a designer, I think of this as the moment of release—when all the hardest parts of trying to listen fall away, and I let myself *go deep into listening*.

I am listening so intently that I jump when someone finally starts to speak, forty minutes into the hour-long meeting. I open my eyes and there is a man in a red flannel shirt. He speaks for a short period, and people listen. They listen in the exact same way they had when they listened to themselves earlier.

After he sits down, a short period of quiet passes before someone else speaks on the same theme, and then another. In Quaker terminology, this is testimony. Those of us in the room are bearing witness to that testimony. Sometimes that testimony can be quite simple and require nothing—for instance, in this meeting the man in red flannel is asking that we all send well wishes to those leading a gun march in Washington that week; this was thoughtful but required minimal action, just a nod of assent from those gathered. Historically, testimony, however, can be quite significant—for instance, the decision to not actively convert people to Quakerism was a testimony delivered in a meeting and it was a testimony that Quakers had to struggle to find the truth in for years and years. The acceptance of that testimony would lead ultimately to the dwindling of the religion.

Later, I tried to break down this listening practice and it seemed to fall into three distinct parts. First, we were asked to practice listening to ourselves, our own inner voice. Those first thirty or so minutes of silence were not, in fact, silence; they were listening to the flow of thoughts through our mind. Second, collectively, we were listening to what was being said when someone rose to give testimony while we were simultaneously listening to ourselves: *How does what I'm hearing relate to what I hear in myself?* Third, in the Quaker tradition, we were asked to listen for a third voice, which happened to be "God's voice." When you mesh your voice with the voice of the person offering testimony, you then listen for divine guidance. That's a pretty sophisticated kind of listening practice; there's no "uh huh, go on" happening here.

Interestingly, this listening practice dovetails with the current psychology thinking on creative processes. Studies of creativity often call out four stages: preparation, incubation, illumination, and verification. An incubation period is defined as a moment of relatively low cognition (i.e., a moment when we're not occupying the mind with complex thinking or behaviors). Research shows that significant new ideas, creative ideas, or breakthrough moments are more likely to happen after incubation periods—and we've all had that moment in the shower when a brilliant notion hits us.

That's because a lot of important things happen during these *supposedly low-cognitive moments.* First, we see the activation of relevant memories: As you sit inside a quiet period, your brain is busy matching the problem or issue up with similar experiences, situations, or patterns in the past. What we commonly call intuition or "trusting our gut" is actually a complex cache of memories: the more of them we have, the more confident our intuition.

Second, and perhaps more interestingly, ideas, patterns, or solutions that we might actually have had that don't find relevant memories begin to lose plausibility. Incubation actually weakens activation of inappropriate solutions. We've all been a victim of what "seemed like a good idea at the time" that actually was nothing of the sort. Listening in an incubate state is asking us to not act.

The last piece of work our mind does while in this low-cognitive state is that it begins to relax self-imposed rules around what a solution or idea might look like. This should make intuitive sense. The more seriously you take a problem, the more likely you are to have a set of rules for how it might be solved. By not actively engaging in problem solving, those rules fall to the background, which actually allows for you to question the appropriateness of the rule set, just as you've been questioning the appropriateness of potential solutions.

The listening practice of the Quakers is, in fact, a "forced incubation." George Papandreou had a similar practice when he was prime minister of Greece. Cabinet meetings were often fractious and uncomfortable, so he decided to begin each one by making his cabinet watch a TED Talk or something else of about the same length. When I asked him how he chose the content to show before each meeting, he replied, "It doesn't matter what the content is, it matters that they listen." He was, in fact, setting the stage for forced incubation. More broadly, organizations that allow teams hours or days of breaks in the middle of a creative process often see significantly more creative outcomes.

So the first, most important, and perhaps hardest rule for creative listening is: Let the words or silence run over you like a shower or the sounds of a stream. Be passive, simply release yourself into whatever the person is or isn't saying. These moments of forced incubation can allow you to discover something great within you, but more important, you might discover something great in someone else.

Step into the Speaker's World

Anthropologists traditionally have lived with subjects for extended periods of time; they become participants in these communities, which helps them understand how they really work and gain true and deep insight. Architecture, the design practice I studied, often gives weight to watching and observing people interacting in a space over asking people about a space. This is what it means to listen with your body.

The goal here is to discover a truth that we may not otherwise glean from just hearing what someone says. We used this participatory listening a lot at IDEO. Our work often begins with a set of in-person interviews in the context in which we're designing for. So, if we're working on consumer financial behaviors, we'll do their bills with them. If we're working on an education project, we might attend class and do homework with a student. I've watched and asked as people work in luxury hotel rooms or tried recuperating in overcrowded hospital rooms. One of my favorite and most simple examples of this happened during an interview with a young woman who was a student at a large university that had hired us. The university had gathered data that its students didn't read. Frankly, the administration was concerned that its entire curriculum would have to be completely rethought.

We were invited into this young woman's apartment and asked her directly, "Do you read?"

"What? No. Never, I just never was much of a reader."

So, the data was right. Students didn't read.

The interview continued, but later, as we were wrapping up, she showed us around the apartment. We walked through her bedroom and were very surprised to see that the walls of her bedroom were covered with shelves bending under the weight of books! The *Twilight* series, *The Hunger Games*, the Sookie Stackhouse series. Really, it seemed, she'd read any series where werewolves and vampires were having sex.

"Oh, wait, it looks like you read," we observed.

"That's not reading"—she was clearly embarrassed—"that's just stupid shit."

She had told us earlier that she didn't read, because the "stupid shit" she did read didn't qualify with what she assumed we must mean when we said reading. Without touring her house, we'd have never discovered the type of reading she did do and that influenced the way we thought of our work going forward.

As it turns out, the serialization of these books is a great model for the design of addictive and engaging curriculum models.

Listening with your body, participating in the context, is so powerful precisely because it removes one of the greatest tools of listening and the greatest potential for bias: the question. Often, as we're articulating the questions we ask in field research, the patterns we think we'll see or the patterns we'd like to see start to get embedded in the question. In these cases, the question can become the enemy of the truth.

Questioning can also be a sign of impatience: Do you like this? Do you do this? Do you think this? Why? Why not? These questions challenge the speaker, or hurry them along, and both are hugely unproductive. When Steve Jobs used to say, "Don't ask," he was really saying don't ask the consumer, because they don't know. When I've had to say, "Don't ask," it's more often because the creative team I'm working with thinks they already know the answer to the question they're asking.

Paul Farmer, the brilliant physician and social activist, tells another great story that illustrates the power of participatory listening. Years ago, he and his colleagues were working to eliminate a deadly form of plague that was killing Haitian children. They discovered quickly the illness was caused by exposure to and ingestion of rat dander, and they assumed that was due to the poor hygiene of village homes. But then Paul spent some time in the infected villages. Most of the homes were quite clean—something the women took great pride in. One morning, as he was observing, he saw the mothers putting on the morning porridge and the grandmothers taking up their willow brooms. In that moment, he saw the true cause of the plague. So vigilant and clean were the villagers that the morning sweep was stirring dust, germs, and rat dander directly into their breakfasts.

Listening with our bodies requires us to listen with all of our senses. It requires us to slow way down and understand the moment and context of you and the person you're listening to over all else.

Don't just observe the surroundings; choose to be in them. Look at the people speaking and try to see and feel what they are feeling. What is their body saying? Are there physical cues that suggest that there is something deeper than what they may be saying? Be aware of discrepancies between what's being said and what's really happening.

In those striking contradictions we discover greater patterns and truths.

Ask for a Story

The truth is, we'll always listen when it's something that we want to listen to. A good story is something we will always make time for. The problem is most people are not good at telling stories, but if you know what makes a good story, you can help them tell one and make them a hero in the process.

The secret here is not that most people are bad storytellers, but rather that there's a secret to getting people to tell good stories.

Think about someone you know who's a fantastic storyteller, who knows how to tell a story that's powerful and impactful, that's just the right length, that really holds you the whole time. For me that was my mother's grandmother. When I was a child, I used to spend weeks, sometimes longer, on my great-grandmother's farm in southern Indiana. She and I were together nonstop, but she was endlessly engaging. One day, as we sat on a wooden swing around sunset, she told me the following story.

During World War II, she worked the night shift in the steel mills. And one morning, after her shift, she'd returned home to her farm and was starting the walk up the long, dusty drive. The sun was just rising, and she was bone-sore, thinking of how she'd now have to spend a couple of hours cooking for the men on the farm.

Suddenly, she saw something on the horizon.

At this point in the story she held up her hands, putting her thumb in front of the now-setting sun. "Slowly," she said, "this thing moved toward me from the sky, blocking out the rising sun." She moved her hands toward me, blocking out more and more of the sun, as she continued. "It got closer and closer, and soon I could see that it was a figure in a blue robe, staring down at me, smiling at me. Finally, this figure was close to me, floating still a couple of feet away, but never closer. He smiled and of course my heart swelled up at the sight of Jesus just feet away. I blinked and rubbed my eyes and he was gone." Her hands opened to the sun. "Now I was tired that day, more than usual, and yet I never felt more strength and more ready to get the daily chores done."

That story became my favorite. I had her repeat it to me over and over again, until I had it memorized. My great-grandmother was a profoundly religious woman, a Christian through and through. She believed she saw God, and that God encouraged her to do work that needed to be done. I'm deeply agnostic and even though I never shared my great-grandmother's beliefs, I came to believe that that experience had been profound for her, it had moved her, shaped her future actions. That, in turn, moved me. I saw the truth in her experience, even if it wasn't mine. The story was so human, so real, that I accepted it at face value despite the fact that it doesn't fit into my belief set.

Think for a moment about that story; it really has four elements that make it work: it's personal, it's short, it's surprising, and it's clarifying.

But we know the other types of storytellers. They wander. They provide too much detail. They're less storytellers than they are narrators. This is where you as the listener can help. When you ask for a story, remember the simplicity of the formula for a story and give the speaker cues.

When people seem to be struggling to share their thoughts with you, to summarize them in a neat way, shift the conversation away from what they think, or did, or believe toward what they felt. Specifically, ask them to tell you a short story. Ask them to show you, through sharing a vivid experience, what they know to be true. So, next time you're listening to someone and they're trying (and failing) to explain their point of view, the next time you find a dialogue arduous, contentious, or confusing, pause and simply ask if they'd tell you a story. Give them guidance too. Ask for a moment that surprised them. Often that's enough.

In situations that are more sophisticated or where you want more nuanced insight, then add more requests for the type of story. Ask a cancer patient, "Tell me a funny story about chemotherapy." Ask a rich person for a story about the last time they felt poor. Ask someone who's recently lost someone for a story about what surprised them most about death. If you're feeling brave, ask them what they thought was funniest about death.

Giving the speaker an interesting frame will help them tell a more interesting story. Helping someone tell you a good story is a mutually rewarding act. It makes the teller a hero and allows you, the listener, to receive greater and more lasting insight into the storyteller and their world.

Get Judgy

Do you want to hear some gossip? Do you want to hear a secret? Talk about our favorite kinds of stories. We love things that are just for us. We're compelled by gossip, fed by it, thrilled by it. We're human, we're insecure, we'd love to know something that only we can know.

But gossip, so often dismissed in content and form, is a legitimate underpinning to any dialogue.

An emergent body of research around a concept called "prosocial gossip" suggests that some gossiping may actually be good for us. The idea is that gossip, in certain contexts, helps us work out who might be predatory in our midst, helps us identify bad actors, and in turn establishes what we believe should be the foundation of social norms for a group.

I saw this firsthand one sweaty afternoon in the jungles of the Amazon. I met a sixty-year-old woman farmer. She had been described to me as an activist who'd helped stop domestic violence in her community. Her weapon: gossip.

As we sat under her mango tree, I asked her how she'd done it. She told me that the mothers of the town used to meet every morning to distribute milk to the village children as a part of a Peruvian nutrition campaign, and of course, they passed the time with local gossip. Through those conversations she was not only able to ascertain the scope of the domestic violence problem but also pinpoint the alpha males in the community—the most self-important men, those with the most machismo and the biggest egos.

(We've seen something similar with the #MeToo movement: For years, for decades, women have spoken inside their own "whisper networks" about the sexual misconduct of famous and ordinary men, and the assaults and harassment they've endured. This was #MeToo in miniature, localized.)

She went to these men, the "alpha males," and spoke with them one on one. She didn't say "beating your wife or daughter is bad," which she knew wouldn't change their behavior. Instead she whispered about other men in the village known for beating their wives: *"Qué gallina, ¿no?"* Which means "Weak, no?" or more accurately "what a wuss." Beating women looks weak, beating women looks cowardly; she was purposefully tapping into the deep cultural constructs of pride, shame, and fear, and in a way, she reprogrammed the prime directive of these men to be anti-abuse advocates. The gossip spread, the lesson was clear, and violence was quelled. She laughed at the simplicity of it.

So what can this mode of conversation teach us about how to be better listeners overall? Gossip is so profoundly powerful precisely because it's a mix between some facts and how we, as individuals, a community, or a crowd, feel about those facts. Gossip asks the listener to make a judgment, to place an overlay of what's right or wrong over what we're hearing. Listening is about judgment, and about hearing judgment in others.

It's OK, in other words, to embrace your feelings as you listen, to respond emotionally and cognitively to what you're hearing. That's only human. But as we become more adept at creative listening, it's important to continuously reflect on and interrogate those feelings and judgments. You're searching not for reaction but for some bit of knowledge, or a sense of truth that offers you a path to proceed.

Making Conversation: Whine and Dine

Now we'll look at how the tenets of creative listening—stories, gossip, incubation, and observation—can be brought together in a way that lets us design a conversation differently.

Throughout most of the creative, strategic, and business worlds, there's a common practice called the focus group. You've probably heard of them. You may even have participated in one. Just in case, let me explain their basic function.

At its heart, it's a research method: you gather a set of people into a room; you place a product or service proposition or an idea into that room; and you ask them to talk about the pros and cons of the offering, if they would buy it, tell someone about it, and so on. This can be a blank conference room with two-way mirrors so subjects can't see the researchers. It might involve very specific types of "consumers"—fifty-two-to-fifty-eight-year-old women going through menopause, new fathers of their first child.

Here's the thing, though: focus groups are deeply flawed. On the surface, getting people together to talk about what they like or don't like about something may seem like a good way to learn, but it's actually quite hard to trust the things you do learn. Eight to twelve people paid to sit in a room and talk about what they do and don't like about something—the structure is completely unnatural to common human interaction.

What that means is you get all kinds of misinformation. You're battling some deeply ingrained pieces of human nature here. First, there's agreeability. We as social humans are not completely comfortable telling someone we don't like something straight to their face; we're inclined toward politeness. We'll say, "I like it; I'm definitely interested in it; I might buy it" because we know that's what you want to hear.

Second, there's fear of judgment. We can't help but want this group of strangers to like us, and we'll respond to prompts with that in mind. We'll say we listen to classical music when we're alone, not Justin Bieber.

Third, by nature we're overly attuned to norms. We'll always try to play up the common characteristics of a group. We'll all talk about how we don't mind changing diapers, or all talk about how much we hate doing it, based on what we think the norm is in that group of first-time fathers.

Unnatural social structures and social interactions create unnatural dynamics, and as people try to conform, they will say things they may not mean. They play a role instead. We can listen to these conversations all day and still not get to the truths we need to uncover. And yet clients keep asking for focus groups. We were stuck in a situation where our clients needed them to believe our research, but we didn't believe in them as a credible source of insight.

So we added wine, lots of wine.

We needed to break down the inhibitions that people had in this unnatural situation and, to be blunt, wine was the easiest way. Wine also signaled something different to these participants, that this was a social setting.

We didn't just add wine, we added lovely invitations that told people they'd be meeting "like-minded" individuals, so they knew the pattern coming in. We put them in social spaces at social times—booths in bars, dining room tables in restaurants, always between 6:00 p.m. and 8:00 p.m.—and just started letting them engage in small talk, so they'd feel less like strangers. We called the gathering Whine and Dine, and asked them to complain about something: their savings account, their constant business travel, how many times they'd been held up in Columbia, you name it. Please complain. We not only removed the stigma around judging—we asked them to judge.

Our designers sat at the dinner table, or in the bar alcove, or a living room and had wine (not as much as the other participants maybe), and listened for the emotional high or low points.

I've heard remarkable things happen at Whine and Dines. During one, a mother told the table how she'd learned to save for her kid's college tuition; all the other women immediately took notes, and so did we. We knew it was accurate because we'd seen the whole emotional arc of the conversation. And what we learned about their savings habits helped us create one of Bank of America's most successful banking products. The participants loved it too; when Whine and Dines were over, attendees often sent us thank-you notes and emails for inviting them to meet up.

The Whine and Dine is an example of making a conversation where almost all of the elements of creative listening are in play. We're asking for short, funny stories over cocktails, no one takes notes. The activity is drinking after work, the conversation is more akin to gossip than it is to sharing insights about a product or service. Listening in on what can seem like gossip and informal chatter opens a door to insight. Letting the conversation run over and through us, watching the dynamics as much as listening to the words, receiving outsize insights rather than confirming our own biases: it's more Bieber than Bach.

Why We Must Listen

Here's the thing: I always assumed that my mother was born a fantastic listener, that her ability to light up people and rooms with her attention was as natural and lucky as being born a painter or a math genius. But as I studied and thought about creative listening, I discovered something that I should have seen far sooner, back when I was sitting with her after her stroke and watching her struggle to follow the most basic arc of a conversation.

Creative listening doesn't just happen. It does take work, a lot of it. That's one thing active listeners get right—they're just wrong about the kind of work it takes. So, this isn't about suddenly making listening easier. It's about making listening better, more fruitful, and often more fun.

Here's how you practice creative listening: Next time you hear someone speaking, practice releasing your judgmental mind and let their words fall over you. Pay attention to what floats to the top. Next time you're sitting with someone whose views you don't understand, ask them for a story. A story that will illuminate their life, that will surprise you, and maybe surprise them. Next time you hear something you disagree with or disturbs you, feel your judgment, and understand where it comes from and what it means. Next time you're with someone whose life is fundamentally different from yours, go with them, ask if you can join them in their lives, and see where that might take you.

And, by the way, you don't have to use every creative listening tool every time you listen.

But if we listen—really, deeply listen—we'll be unburdened from the frankly boring kind of listening we've been doing up until today. We won't just be waiting impatiently for things we already know or believe. We won't be listening primarily for the speaker's benefit—but for our own. We'll discover things in what people are saying, or how they are saying it, that can change us or help us solve our own problems or inspire new ideas for ourselves.

One thing I've learned from trying to listen more like my mother: it doesn't solve everything, but it certainly makes everything more interesting.

Conversation Break: Illuminations

In the Middle Ages, and long before the printing press, there were illuminated manuscripts, arduously but exquisitely hand-written texts. Some were religious in nature, some offered tales of courtly life, and embedded throughout were small images called "illuminations." These illuminations mattered: literacy rates were low and the images that accompanied could entertain those who couldn't read and provide guidance and support for those who could but still needed help. When I studied medieval manuscripts in college and would gingerly leaf through an ancient book with linen gloves on, these small and enticing illuminations would delight and surprise me.

I have talked about the idea of "asking for a story," but let's dive deeper.

Think of stories like those small, simple, delightful illuminations that help people understand you more completely. Providing these moments of illumination is integral to the ability to engage and connect with people you're in conversation with. They are the moments that will provide insight into you and ultimately provide the basis for empathy building.

It's important for you to get good at asking for stories, but it's equally important that you tell stories that are the very best they can be. I like to call these kinds of stories "illuminations." They don't recount every moment of an event in chronological detail; instead they are concise, compressed, and highly concentrated narratives that capture the essence of a memory or an experience. They create, in other words, a picture that captures a thousand words—they are told with intention; they are designed to carry meaning, to engage, and perhaps even to instruct by illuminating a facet of human experience.

For years I've worked with designers and clients, helping them illuminate their work, their message, their philosophy and design principles through this approach. I try to do the same with my own work (and even in the pages of this book), and certainly when I'm trying to "make" conversations with others. When I shift my most important lived experiences to great stories—illuminations—I typically use four principles:

1. AN ILLUMINATION SHOULD BE SHORT

You've probably been with someone who tells you a story and it winds and meanders and includes literally everything that happened. You yourself might do that. Often, when I find myself telling a story and I'm suddenly aware that it's gone on for fifteen minutes, I realize it's not a story at all, I'm just recounting my life. That's fine when you need to vent or decompress, but a story in the context of dialogue and conversation making has to be crisp, economical, and well parsed.

These stories have a purpose: to share something about you and your view of the world. So, start by looking at the stories you tell all the time, and see how you can edit them down to their essence. Try turning a fifteen-minute interlude into a three-minute story.

2. AN ILLUMINATION SHOULD SUGGEST AN EMOTIONAL RESPONSE

This is important. An illumination should evoke an emotion in the listener, crystallizing in them something that you felt. My favorite kind of story is usually a funny one. I just find people tend to remember funny, or at the least are open to hearing a funny story more than once.

But it can be sad, it can convey hardship. It can be anything that helps the listener understand you and how you feel. It's easy to pinpoint the emotion in a story once you start asking yourself what the pervading emotion is. As you review the stories you tell often—or the ones you think are particularly illuminating about you, your values, and your life—first make sure they indeed have an emotional core. If you can't simply spot the predominant emotion in a story, then dig deeper.

3. AN ILLUMINATION SHOULD START WHERE IT STOPS

Know the ending of the story before you start telling it. Too often, we think that we must recount the entire process or lead up to an event in order to impress listeners. It's the equivalent of having to listen to someone recount their day, minute by minute. It's not interesting. It's not illuminating, either.

A story needs to end, and an illumination ends when you discover the insight, not when you finish something. Find the truly revelatory piece of your story and make that where your story stops.

4. AN ILLUMINATION SHOULD HAVE A TWIST WITH A REVEAL

The stories we are likely to remember most tend to hold some kind of surprise or revelation at their core: "That's why no one wanted her to buy a lottery ticket!" "Oh, I knew he shouldn't have had that glass of amontillado!"

The reason we read them—and the reason we all go nuts for *The Twilight Zone* and *Black Mirror*—is we love surprises; we love the twist. Some of the elements above help you practice finding twists. Stop your stories before they're done; stop them when the realization happens; stop when the emotion of the story takes a sudden shift from sad to funny, funny to scary. Find your twist and make it the end point for your story.

The story I told about my great-grandmother had all four components. First, it was short, I retell it to this day, and it takes a minute. Second, it conveyed multiple emotions—exhaustion, loss, and hope. Third, she knew where the ending was, and her revelation packed a punch: "It was Jesus!" Enough said.

That story sticks with me today, nearly forty-five years after I first heard it, because it illuminated some things about my great-grandmother—her faith, her dedication, and her belief that her work was special.

Use illuminations to help people understand you in the moments when there may be friction or a lack of connection. Use these illuminations when it's important to build an emotional link and deeper insight into why you feel the way you do; use them when you need to overcome difference. Sharing these kinds of stories will help you get through conversations that scare you, and they will help others understand you.

CHAPTER 3

CLARITY

> When we learn new words and ideas, and
> then begin to see them everywhere, the world
> is suddenly more legible and more vivid.
> Language reveals to us what was always there,
> but to what before we may have simply passed
> over, we now feel intimately connected.
>
> —*Meara Sharma*

I once spent three days in the Himalayas with a set of spiritual and cultural leaders brought together to discuss cultural institutions and how they could play a role creating connection in divided communities. The location was significant because you don't just open your Uber app and head to the Himalayas; it's an emotional and logistical investment to go that far and that high.

The title of the symposium was "Art and Empathy."

The group in conversation used the word *empathy* loosely;

the conversation shifted fluidly back and forth between "empathy" and "compassion." At first, no one took note. At the end of the second day, however, it became apparent that some people in the room used the word *empathy* in a particular way; another group used the word *compassion* in a different, equally particular way. We were not, as it seemed at first, using the two words interchangeably. Indeed, we were divided: two groups talking about two different words.

When we finally got to defining the terms more clearly, we unveiled a deep disagreement over the motivations and goals of the people in the room. What had seemed like semantics turned out to be a difference in ideology.

The end of the second day of any conversation is way too late to make a discovery like this. Much of the last precious day was spent trying to see if the group could redefine *empathy* so that they could agree on an outcome to the convening. We were unable to get to a collective and common definition of the term, and the session ended inconclusively with its participants completely divided.

When I looked back at my invitation to "Art and Empathy," I realized that the word *empathy* was never defined; its meaning was assumed. Unfortunately, conversations often fail fast due to just this sort of lack of clarity.

Sometimes words fail us because we don't have a shared understanding of their meaning. We assume that everyone has a common understanding of the words and concepts we're discussing, when in truth we do not. Sometimes we may be using language that's purpose-built for a specific conversation but not well suited to the next conversation we're about to have.

Language is how we express ideas, so common language affects not only what we say but where we go and the ideas we build together. Our goal in making conversation is to be certain that the words we use, the language we speak, and the concepts we explore are clear and understood by all.

Defining Our Words

As my experience in the Himalayas shows, language is tricky. There is an inexactness in language, even when we speak the same language. Especially among well-intentioned, highly motivated people, we frequently assume that we share the same assumptions, values, and goals. The impulse to assume the best can put productive conversations at risk, especially when the conversation is based on values and personal experiences. Our differences may not be obvious at first, which is why these words require explication, translation, and often redefinitions.

ESTABLISHING MEANING

One way to make sure we're clear on the meanings behind the words we use is to set our terms and definitions up front.

If we had started with a clear and established meaning for *empathy* before we embarked for the Himalayas, some people might have decided not to make the journey, but everyone there would have known what they were working for.

The notion of establishing meaning sounds like it could be pedantic and time-consuming. But it's not—it's assertive and often provides momentum to move forward. When you find yourself in a conversation that is centered on a singular word or term, a term that is essential to the topic, establish its meaning *early*. Struggles over words and definitions often reveal a deeper struggle—not only about words, but about ideas. Figure out whether the issue is semantic or ideological, fast. Establishing meaning, helping people get clear on key words or terms up front is fundamental to helping them understand whether this is a conversation they should be committing to in the first place. My approach to this is "Assert and Agree."

When words really matter, define your terms straightforwardly. Assert a definition and ask that people agree to that definition for the duration of the conversation. Go to a common and collective resource. Not to sound like a sixth grade teacher, but dictionaries still exist, and that's a good thing. Share the standard dictionary definition, and then ask the room to agree to that definition at the outset.

If you are designing dialogue with terms that have some potential to cause confusion, conflict, or disagreement, take the time to define them even before entering that dialogue. If the group can't agree, the question becomes: "Is this the right conversation for them?" In clarifying the key terms up front you are also giving participants a valuable tool to assess their commitment to the dialogue.

If we had seen a definition of the word *empathy* before we went to the Himalayas, the conversation that ensued would have been different. Based on a simple definition source—a definition culled from a dictionary—disagreements would have been impossible to ignore. Asking people to agree to a definition beforehand might have made the assembly smaller, but the results more satisfying to everyone. Establishing meaning through "Assert and Agree" surfaces differences and ultimately leads to group commitment.

EXTRACTING MEANING

The other way is to continuously explore and excavate hidden meanings, the beliefs and biases that linger in the background and sometimes hang in the air. This investigative process is about pulling the hidden meaning behind what we say forward into the conversation.

Think about a word you use frequently. One of my favorites is *inspiration* or *inspirational*. But I need to get better about clarifying what I mean when I say the word.

If you say something like "I need inspiration" or if you hear someone say "let's get some inspiration," that word does not have enough to stand on its own; it needs more context. We may find out that our idea of inspiration is not aligned when it's too late: I might have been thinking of a Hudson Valley landscape painting, whereas everyone else was thinking of a TED Talk they heard the day before. They're both forms of inspiration, but they're both pretty different.

Words like this pop up in conversations more than we realize. When you say the word *revolution*, are you thinking about the French one or the introduction of the iPhone? When you hear the word *creative*, do you have an image in your mind of a painter in her studio or do you see a team brainstorming in a conference room? Neither is wrong, but they are different, and that difference matters.

These kinds of words are deceptive; when we use them, we assume we all agree about what *ethical, inspirational,* or *creative* means but the meanings can be remarkably different. Not only that, but the meaning behind the words is rich with potential for building connections between our differences. Humanizing these words by sharing our personal backstories enriches discussions and encourages learning.

Extracting meaning, as opposed to establishing it through the more tactical "Assert and Agree" approach, is gentler, subtler and more playful. When you find words coming up often in a conversation, the practice of extracting meaning allows you to delve deeper, to probe participants for anecdotes and examples that reveal what these phrases personally mean to them. You might also encourage people to bring words to life by sharing visuals and images with the group.

GETTING VISUAL ... WITH WORDS

I'm not asking you to draw. Well, not really. But showing a strategy—envisioning what that strategy looks like in action—can catalyze a common vision. So, for instance, when you want to develop a shared vision, why not take the word *vision* seriously and flesh out that image? Draw a picture. If you're in a conversation with someone where a word is coming up a lot, ask yourself if there is a visual that comes to mind when you hear that word. If you do, it's likely that others do as well. Pause and ask the question: "When you say inspiration, what does that look like?"

When you draw a picture to convey meaning, you're forced to be specific. It's harder to misunderstand what someone means if they draw a picture.

Even if your terms and language don't immediately evoke

a visual element, consider adding language that does. A visual can take something quite complex and somewhat mystifying and familiarize it.

Great public speakers are experts at using visual language to simplify complex topics and issues. Alas, it's also true that those who aren't clear on their meanings may also rely on visuals to hide that fact, but that, too, can provide important information about the gaps in understanding that may put the conversation at risk.

For a while there was a wine store in Chicago called Valhalla where I used to send people to understand the power of visual language.

Many people are intimidated by wine stores, but almost everybody is afraid of the sommelier. A sommelier, after all, has mastery of a very specialized, very intimidating language, the language of wine. Wine words—technical terms like *malolactic* or *tannins*—just don't exist in everyday language. More confusing, seemingly everyday words like *breathing* or *brilliant* don't mean the same things to sommeliers as they do in our daily lives.

Good sommeliers, the ones who try to be the least intimidating, will strive to use simple language that evokes images and flavors. Good sommeliers will never say the word *malolactic*; instead they will use a word like *buttery* or *creamy* to describe what a wine might taste like. Buttery is the opposite of intimidating. I have a friend who is quite good at translating wine language, and it's not uncommon for her to use phrases like "cat pee" or "wet dog" to describe a wine. It's funny (and sometimes disgusting, yes), but it's definitely not intimidating.

That language, visual and suggestive of how something might taste, is a good start. But the wine store Valhalla took it a bit further. The owners recognized that even descriptive words that wine people use can be confusing and off-putting to the rest of us. The word *earthy* suggests what a wine might taste like, but it's hard to discern if that's a flavor you'd actively seek out (never mind cat pee). Valhalla got rid of this kind of language altogether. They replaced the language of wine with a language that most of their shoppers seemed to understand better, the language of celebrities.

If you were shopping there, you might find yourself in front of a bottle of rosé topped with a handwritten card that might say something like: This wine is like Britney Spears, light, fresh, cheap, and surprisingly fun to drink. A bottle of red wine might have a card beneath it that said: This wine is like Madonna, sinewy, tawny, and aging well.

This might seem absurd. But replacing the language of wine with the language of *People* magazine made the wine store easy to navigate—in fact, a complete delight.

Applying evocative visual language can be used whenever you're trying to extract and establish meaning.

TELLING STORIES ABOUT WORDS

Words like *ethics, values, power,* and, yes, *empathy* are not simple and straightforward words; they have remarkably nuanced modes of interpretation based on where you sit in culture, class, and context. These are also words where asking for a visual isn't really going to clarify much. I don't think I could easily come up with an image for the word *empathy*.

If you want precision around these types of words, dictionary definitions will not suffice. So don't ask for a definition, ask for an example. Ask for a story. (Are you already getting sick of this instruction? Well, asking for a story is a piece of advice I'm going to return to again and again in this book because it's so intuitive and so useful.)

Frequently, when I'm first working with a group and starting the conversation in earnest, I ask everyone to introduce themselves and share a personal experience that relates to that term or concept.

A few years ago, I worked with a diverse group of people who had come together to identify how they might develop a new learning experience for teens. While we may intuitively get the idea of what learning means, when you're talking about developing a new learning experience, the word *learning* can be a liability. Learning has surprisingly different meanings depending on who you are and how traditional—or not—your idea of learning might be.

At our first meeting, I asked everyone to introduce themselves by telling a short story of one of their most impactful learning experiences.

The stories were, as expected, varied.

One person told a story of having to teach their twenty-something child how to prepare their taxes and how that experience forced her to get really clear on the nuances of filing taxes, things she thought she knew but it turned out she wasn't completely sure about.

Someone else related a story about her mother teaching her to drive, and the stress of driving on real streets. Actually, a lot of people told stories with the same theme—stories about learning that weren't easy, pleasant, or free of stress.

On the surface, everybody's story was different, but several common themes emerged. By the time we'd completed introductions, we knew each other better and how our personal experiences had led us to this moment. We also had developed a set of themes that gave us insight and background about what kind of learning we would be talking about.

Identifying those themes becomes even more valuable than simple definitions of key words. These themes become touchstones as the conversation progresses. As you discuss, say, a new learning experience the group might want to put into the world, you can hark back to these themes as a way to ground the conversation in a common vocabulary. When someone says *learning*, you can push further about what kind of learning, referring to the themes and root stories that motivated the group in the first place.

So try to make sure that you've established the definitions of tricky terms before the conversation even begins. You'll lower the obstacles that might stand in the way of making conversation and help people decide that they want to be in the conversation in the first place.

Essentially, what we're doing here is building a glossary.

Gather and collect the key terms you use in a conversation. These terms will be critical to building a common language. Use visuals to make sure everyone has a similar picture in mind. Try short personal stories that help us make a human connection to abstract words or concepts. Keep track of all the references:

visuals and stories that come up as a way to define language become a rich background to the conversation being had.

Talk Normal

The search for simple, clear, shared language is only the first step in gaining clarity. One must also be on the alert for language that, intentionally or not, obfuscates meaning and excludes participation.

I often lead groups of highly trained specialists who are accustomed to using special language that reflects their expertise and the complexity of the subject matter at hand (law, management, consulting, medicine, and even my own profession of architecture). It can be a bit of a shock at first when I admonish them to "talk normal"—that is, to express their expertise in the simplest terms possible—for the rest of us.

I once worked with a small hospital in Missouri that was committed to being recognized both for patient care and patient experience. The key to fixing that patient experience, they believed, was fixing waiting times and their patients' experience of waiting.

In hospitals, patients wait everywhere—in reception areas, on exam tables, and in hallways. When you talk to patients, they seem resigned to waiting, reluctantly accepting the fact that getting medical care in a hospital is a complicated, all too bureaucratic process. For most people, though, it isn't the waiting that makes them unhappy; it's the anxiety of not knowing why they're waiting or what they're waiting for. Here again, words matter.

The word in question for those seeking hospital treatments? *Triage*.

Triage is the process medical professionals use for classifying the urgency of an injury or illness. It comes from the French word for sifting. It's a critical step hospital staff use to assess how urgent your need is, and what the next step in your treatment will be. But if you ask patients in an emergency room what triage is, only about half the people in the room can define it. The triage process is not only necessary, it's a good thing for patients. But because the term isn't familiar to most, it won't be clear to them why some patients wait for hours to receive care while others who arrive later are whisked into treatment.

Specialized language can be problematic: On the one hand, it creates affinity and loyalty among groups who have been trained and educated to understand its special meanings and use these terms in their work. At the same time, it denies access to the very people meant to be helped by this expertise. All too often it includes a few and excludes many.

And don't get me started on all those medical acronyms—EKGs, CPR, BP, AIDS, ADHD, and so on. Acronyms are the hallmark of bureaucracy. They inspire cynicism in organizations that are overly reliant on them. And let's be honest: no one is ever proud to share a new acronym.

So let's stop using them. They universally shut down conversations with anyone outside of the circle of people deeply embedded in that culture and language. At the very least, use the full name for the acronym, say all the words it stands for or, even better, find other words altogether. Don't be lazy; don't be rude. And if you are on the receiving end of an acronym, never hesitate to ask someone to spell it out: "Remind me, what does _____ stand for again?" That is a perfectly legitimate request when faced with a word salad, whether it is intentionally or accidentally exclusionary.

Anyway, here's the thing: doctors, nurses, and hospital staff need language and terminology that allows them to communicate quickly and efficiently in complex and fast-moving situations. When health-care professionals are working with other health-care workers—or, say, when lawyers are talking with other lawyers—they should by all means use whatever language works. But when they step out of these circles, it's time to lose the lingo. When you or a loved one is discussed in a language that is not built for you, it can be hard to keep track of the conversation and still assert your agency in the interaction.

In the case of the hospital I was advising, we were able to decrease patient anxiety and unhappiness by teaching hospital staff when to "talk normal." Words such as _assess_ and _evaluate_ replaced _triage_. While perhaps not as precise, the new lingo made sense to patients. Nowadays, when you enter the emergency room at that Missouri hospital, you see a triage nurse . . . sitting under a sign saying: "Start Here."

Or look at another example, from my own field of architecture. The architectural term _intervention_ can literally mean everything from a bench, an exhibit, a hallway, a window. Almost anything can be considered an architectural intervention. Fine, let architects love their interventions, but if you want to engage real people, why not call it a bench or a window or a hallway? (I was heartened to learn that these days architects are debating the use of the term *intervention*, wondering whether it is too obscure to be useful.)

Talking normal matters most when you're interacting with groups with creative differences—those of mixed disciplines, mixed background, and varying degrees of depth in the topic being discussed. You can decide to talk normal, be less fancy, and increase your persuasiveness and influence. That's the point after all, isn't it?

SIMPLE LANGUAGE FOR HARD CONCEPTS

In 2009 my IDEO colleagues and I were hired by a consortium of Peruvian political organizations to look at the problem of low voter turnout in national and local elections. The problem was especially troubling because voting is mandatory in Peru. If citizens don't vote, they could be fined or even lose their citizenship status.

We spent time in the capital city of Lima, as well as in more rural communities in the Andes Mountains and the Amazonian jungles. We met with teachers in their classrooms, farmers in the fields, and political activists on the street. Almost all of them were politically sophisticated. Surprisingly, though, almost none of them voted. They uniformly felt that the political discourse in the country was too complicated to understand, and that resulted in an uncertainty about how to vote. Faced with this uncertainty, they chose to opt out of voting altogether.

Political language can be complicated, but policy solutions and ballot measures felt like they took simple ideas and made them even more complicated. For the Peruvians we talked to, "complicated" equaled "corruption." Complex concepts seemed like a way to obscure bad and perhaps even corrupt behavior and to skirt the country's real problems. For the people we spoke with, one just needed to look around to see what the real issues were. The quality of the education was poor; in fact, almost anyone could set up a school in their garage. The police were corrupt. Police in the capital city, Lima, routinely issued tickets that were no more than formalized bribes. The problems seemed apparent to everyone—even to visitors like us—so why did politicians speak about them in such complex, confusing language?

One of the solutions that came out of the project was a simple sticker campaign with the words "Fix this" or "Arreglen esto" on them. The idea was that people could point to issues that mattered through direct, simple language and direct, simple concepts. You didn't need policy language or political analysis, you could just say, "Fix this."

The clients—nonprofits looking for a simple way to invigorate political conversation—were certain that Peruvians would never resort to a sticker campaign as a way to express themselves. But when we launched a pilot test in the Andean city of Cuzco, the stickers disappeared so fast we were worried we might have lost them. And then we began to find these stickers all over the city. "Fix this" was stuck on the doors of schools or on classroom desks. Police officers slapped them on each other's backs as a joke, or pasted them on the backs of squad cars, like bumper stickers.

Taking the complexity out of politics with normal language

was not only easy but liberating and energizing for these cit-izens. "Fix this" was a clear request for action. In fact, putting a "Fix this" sticker on something that was broken was not a conversation at all; it was in itself an action.

When we do the work of translating and simplifying com-plex terminology, we allow people to see their agency in the process—to take responsibility for joining and shaping the con-versation and for turning words into action.

BUILD SIMPLE STRUCTURES

You likely last wrote a haiku in grade school. So just to remind you, a haiku is a very short form of poetry that comes out of Japanese literary tradition. It contains no more than seventeen syllables—syllables, not words. There are five syllables in the first line, seven in the second, and five again in the third. A good haiku must contain two contrasting or complementary ideas; the "cut" between the two ideas is meant to create a more vivid and clear image. A haiku must be simple yet self-contained; it's like the beautiful, rich, and inspiring ancestor of the tweet.

While traditionally haiku are often about nature or spir-ituality, you find them everywhere. For example, the British business magazine *Real Business* once had an open stream that asked CEOs to describe their businesses in a haiku format:

> Data can be gold
> If not used for decisions
> It's worth less than coal
> —Rado Kotorov

Or the Kellogg School of Management, which asked leadership development professionals to send their best lessons in business leadership in the haiku form. Kellogg then published the haiku in their online journal:

> Company Culture
> It must be actively shaped
> Or it shapes itself
> —Maor Cohen

Both of the examples above give clear and vivid descriptions of business practices and business models. You can understand the core of what Kotorov's business is without knowing anything else about it. You get Cohen's lesson on leadership without the need of a book on leadership to support it.

Think about what you want to communicate and whether you can translate it into a haiku. You want it simple and short, you want some form of comparison that allows you to clarify what you're trying to communicate, and you want a basic standalone structure.

Don't take your complex ideas and turn them into a tweet—that's obnoxious.

Do take your complex ideas and put them into poetry. It takes five minutes of thinking at the maximum, but the work it does to essentialize what you're saying is useful to your thinking and clarifying for others in the room. If you don't want to read the rest of this chapter, just make sure to read the following haiku instead:

Simplicity in words
Context in concepts will
Lead to clarity
—FRED DUST

It's not beautiful, but it is clarifying.

If everyone in a room tries to write a haiku about what they're discussing in the same five minutes, you build a context and landscape for the ideas being discussed. The work is both to simplify and structure your thinking, conveying something richer and more resonant to the person who hears your new form. Take the essence of what a haiku offers and consider using it to clarify your ideas.

You can use this practice anytime you want to have clarity about what you're talking about. Restate key concepts in simplified forms and be creative with the formats you use. You can try imposing a rigid structure—there are endless possibilities! Try a two-word description, or a diagram, or even a cartoon.

Give It a Name

There are many ways to go about naming a child. For some, choosing a name to honor family members is important. For others, choosing a name that reflects cultural traditions and values is critical. Still others seek novelty and recombination, creating entirely new names and new sounds. All are aimed at giving a name to someone with a promising future.

We name our kids, our cars, our boats. Why not take the

same care with our projects—whether it's naming a new initiative, a new product, or a new division?

I started seriously thinking about naming conventions when I was working as an architect. At one point looking at new classroom models for Stanford University, we witnessed a common but interesting behavior as students exited the classroom. Regardless of how the classroom conversation had gone—whether it was lecture-based or the Socratic method—we noticed that the dynamic between teachers and students was always lively and energetic as they headed out the door. Bags in hand, in a narrow doorway, suddenly students who had been nonverbal for ninety minutes would open up and ask hard questions of their professors on the way out the door.

We decided to create a space for those conversations—a small space just outside the classroom. In order to justify the space, because it took space away from the classroom itself, we had to explain the kind of activity that the space would enable. We ended up calling the space the "front porch." Very quickly the client, Stanford University, and other key stakeholders began to adopt that term.

At the time, I thought that the name was primarily useful as a way of understanding whether people believed in the idea, and it was. Over the years, however, I realized that the name worked on other levels. Yes, it described the space; yes, it lent a visual component to an idea; but it also described the kinds of conversation that Stanford wanted to encourage to happen there. It established an intent.

Since then I've become relentless about names.

Names should describe what things do and what they mean. Names should describe how things feel or might feel. Names can even describe how you should act when you engage with these things and, most important, names clarify intent.

I've encouraged designers to name concepts that they've designed. I've encouraged organizations to give names to the initiatives they are proud of, businesses to consider how names can ground things for their customers and how naming a conversation can affect what happens in that conversation.

I often ask individuals to think of names for the goals or outcomes that matter most to them. But it can be rewarding to do that work as a collective. Naming something together as a group is more than an exercise in clarification; it also builds commitment and connection, both essential to transformational dialogue.

You can even name a conversation. Naming a conversation tells people what kind of conversation it is.

I was once halfway through a series of meetings that I had called "Business Forensics" when I realized what a terrible name it was. The gatherings and conversations were dour and serious. It shouldn't have been a surprise; you do forensics on things that die or things that fail. Forensics has a specific intent.

When it occurred to me that the name might be the thing that was setting this negative tone for the exploration, I shifted the name of the conversations from "Business Forensics" to "Business Fitness." The tone of the very next meeting shifted from downbeat to upbeat, from problem-focused to solution-focused; it engineered a whole different conversation.

In retrospect, both names were of value. The forensic part

of the conversation, while somber, did suggest that there was a lot of work to be done on diagnosing what was going wrong. The shift in name to "fitness" marked a transition in intent just at the right moment. It was now time for decisions, new habits, and action. While renaming the conversation had not been intentional, the two names indicated both the activity and the mood appropriate to the different stages. The name shifted the outcome.

This example of naming a conversation captures what I mean by clarity. While "Business Fitness" is a name, it really is an expression of a concept. Using simple, understandable terms, "Business Fitness" tells you exactly what the conversations will strive to do; in the same way, it provides a guide to the tone those conversations will have. It's interesting to note that while "Business Forensics" was something done by a few people, "Business Fitness" was picked up by the entire organization. It described a concept that everyone felt like they could participate in.

SET SEARCH TERMS

Establishing a collective language begins to define what you're looking for. Establishing search terms creates visions of a future state, and they can help a group navigate an otherwise unclear exploration. We fixate on what is relevant to us, and we see what we want to see.

About fifteen years ago I got a call from a senior executive at the Ritz-Carlton. They wanted to develop a new service practice that they could roll out across their system. Specifically, they wanted a service experience that a guest would feel, but not necessarily put their finger on, something you couldn't quite articulate. This was in an era when other hotels were branding their sleep experiences or inviting celebrity chefs to run their restaurants. Starwood's "Heavenly Bed" had swept the industry—a great example, by the way, of the power of a good name. In a moment when everyone was watching for a competitive move, Ritz-Carlton wanted a service experience to be tangible but too subtle to be copied.

It would have seemed impossible, if they hadn't given this nonexistent service model a name.

These executives were calling the service initiative "scenography," despite the fact that they had no idea what they meant by the word. Scenography typically refers to stagecraft in the theater, but in this case, they wanted nothing that was staged, no scripts, and they certainly did not want it to be too easily recognizable. The name was so compelling because it hinted at the potential of a solution. The name hinted at a vision; it suggested to us the characteristics, if not the final form, of the thing we were looking for.

Here's the thing: When we started looking for scenography, we found it everywhere. Subtle compositions of furniture and objects, the right music in the background, the moment all the candles were lit in a room felt like what scenography was supposed to mean.

We were able to build the system, and true to that very first conversation we called it "Scenography." The organization loved it and soon scenography was being talked about everywhere. From general managers to housecleaners, Ritz-Carlton employees understood scenography and wanted to have the chance to try it. To this day, if I walk into a Ritz and ask to see their scenography, employees' faces will light up and they'll happily tour you through their specially crafted moments.

These executives intuited something profound about language when they named their goal. They could have called the project Ritz-Carlton Service Standards or used the acronym RCSS for short—after all, that's what scenography was. Instead they called it "Scenography" because it implied more than standards. It sounded creative, inspiring, and fun. Most important, once you heard the word, you couldn't help but look for it. Scenography was sticky not just because it suggested the work to be done, but because it inspired a way of seeing. It showed us what to look for, what to search for.

So can the right words in a conversation.

I was once in a group of people struggling with the issue of how to come up with solutions for communities facing financial collapse. We were all a bit lost until Muhammad Yunus, the Nobel Peace Prize winner, introduced the idea of "Compassionate Commerce." He never actually defined the term; the term defined itself.

In the conversation, we had been pivoting back and forth between market-based solutions and more traditional philanthropic solutions. The concept of "Compassionate Commerce" united that exploration. When you put the two words together, compassion and commerce, they suggested a whole other landscape of ideas or systems to pursue. Nothing will be purely market driven, but philanthropy could be used to jump-start enterprise and economies.

The concept of Compassionate Commerce propelled us forward; it did so by giving a name to our intent, to what we had been searching for. Compassionate Commerce became our search term. The phrase gave us parameters to investigate, if not the exact solution. Once we started using it, we started to see it, to reckon with the task of bringing the concept into being. It set our intention.

When you name something, you are establishing a narrative. A name can set a story in motion. Naming something together is a fundamentally optimistic act. Naming something means that the group believes something should exist in the world. Pull names from analogues to outcomes you want to have. Make sure your name isn't just descriptive of what something is but descriptive of the aspiration you have for it. Keep track of the name and whether people adopt it, as it becomes an indicator of whether people accept and connect to the idea it stands for.

DON'T MASK INTENT

Clarity is foundational to making conversation, and the words we use are essential to that clarity. But sometimes seeking the definition of a word or term can end a conversation altogether. Words matter, but words don't matter enough to lose hours or days over.

Hopefully by now you've seen both the reward and the risk in thinking deeply about language. Consider, for example, the recent United Nations' declaration of World Oceans Day. As explained to me by one oceanographer, the declaration had been a long time coming. Indeed, the ocean science community had made the request for a day of global need for ocean health in 1995. Twenty years later, the UN was ready to declare the observance of the day.

The problem was that over the last twenty years the Ocean Literacy movement—a group of scientists focused on helping people like us understand the complexity of what's currently happening with the oceans of the world—had shifted their language. They no longer used the word *oceans* but rather *ocean* to express the interconnectedness of the world's water system. This small shift had a relatively big impact on the way laypeople began to understand their local impact on a global issue. And that shift had taken years to become commonplace in the dialogue around ocean health.

When they got the notice from the United Nations that they were going to finally declare World Oceans Day, they thought for a moment about trying to correct the language but almost immediately decided to let it go. In the words of that oceanographer, they "didn't want to sacrifice a day for a word."

Yet I've seen many people sacrifice more than a day for a word—getting caught up and knocked off track by endless digressions about terminology.

So don't get carried away. Work for simplicity, translate whatever is possible from sophisticated terminology to simple language, give important things good names, and don't be afraid to try different language to see if it gives you a new perspective on a topic. Words matter, but they don't matter enough to destroy positive outcomes or to bog down the creation of strong communities of action. Think carefully, be intentional, but don't judge words so harshly that the tail starts wagging the dog.

Making conversation requires creative solutions, but as this chapter has shown, being too clever in your use of language is beside the point. That's why I often suggest that groups forget about finding the perfect phrase or wording, and instead work toward the simplest articulation of their desired outcome. Don't be clever. Don't be fancy. Once you've gained clarity on common terms and language, you can use the methods I've outlined here to settle on the goals you're trying to achieve.

Remember, too: the tools we've established here can be used throughout an engagement. Whenever a conversation feels like it's going astray, check to see if something has gone wrong with the language itself. Interrupting a conversation to collectively refine and define terms, stopping to play with simplification, or taking a few minutes to name ideas and goals can also help realign participation around the same topic.

That is how creative tensions get resolved and conversations are made. More important, it's how conversations can become the fuel of lasting change and progress.

Conversation Break: Script Spotting

In the realm of film, television, and theater, scripts dictate what is said, but also describe characters and the plot. Similarly, you may encounter people in daily life—a politician, a corporate leader—who seem to speak as if reading from a script or even, occasionally, seem to "go off script" by saying something impromptu or surprisingly personal.

Scripts exist, too, in other places and other spaces; they may not be written down, they may not even be formed from words, but nevertheless they offer guidance and cues about how we should act and what we can expect from others. Here are three of the most common places where you might encounter a script that you might not have noticed.

1. SPACES

Many spaces have a script embedded in them—an implication of the kind of conversation that should happen in them and even the roles that should be played. Sometimes that's purposeful and you should think about what that purpose is. A courtroom is an extreme example: it is purpose-built for the conversation that is to be had—every part of a courtroom has both symbolic meaning and specific roles associated with it. The judge's elevated bench suggests authority and ownership; the witness stand next to the judge facing out to the room is both protected by authority and attended to by all; the jury box typically on the side facing the entirety of the room makes them both witness and audience. The space is built to support the script of a trial.

"Scripted spaces" are not usually as formal as a courtroom. The design of your living room, for instance, is quite different from the design of your office and its conference rooms.

With my training as an architect, I'm attentive to the script in a space: how the design of a home or office or a place of formal proceedings facilitates (or not) purposeful conversations. Intuitively, we all respond to the cues embedded in these spatial scripts—where to sit, how to conduct oneself, whether it's OK to lie down or sit up. So, in this way, purpose-built spaces become another tool for fostering creative conversations. And, of course, the wrong space, or spaces not well thought out, can also make conversations more difficult and less productive.

2. RULES

Another script that is subtle but often as common is rules, be they explicit or implicit. Rules can be purposeful and are often placed into conversations as a way of guiding that conversation, appropriate input, and desired outcome. Sometimes these rules can be preexisting and quite formal, meant to keep decorum and structure. Perhaps the most famous example is *Robert's Rules of Order*, which is broadly used for board meetings despite the fact that they were written nearly two hundred years ago—albeit continuously revised. Sometimes these rules can be developed on the spot as "agreements" that are set before a conversation, which are established more as a way of guiding the tone of a conversation and providing a sense of safety in that conversation.

Both those examples are places where rules are explicitly put into place and stated. It's as important to look for places where there are unstated rules. A therapy session, for instance, has perhaps unstated rules about the way a conversation should proceed. For example, it's appropriate and expected that a therapist will ask highly personal and probing questions and it's equally inappropriate for the patient to ask the same kinds of questions back.

The key is to look for rules that may dictate a conversation when it's unclear who put them in place or for what reason. Interestingly, we often forget over time why those rules are in place, so you may find yourself governed by rules that make no sense for the conversation you're participating in. I saw this at IDEO where it could often feel like the treasured rules of brainstorming had infiltrated all of our conversations despite the fact that they often prohibited the other kinds of conversations we needed to have.

Start looking for conversations and the rules that are put in place to guide them; they will truly pop up all over. As we'll see later, rules are constraints and, as such, they are one of the most powerful guide sets for the conversations we will have.

3. TEXTS

Sometimes scripts show up in a way that's very similar to the way scripts appear as a kind of background blueprint for a play or a TV show—quite literal texts. Turn to the back of any Oprah's Book Club selection, or for that matter any book taught in schools, and you'll often find a "discussion guide," a set of questions to be used to lead a group through a conversation on the topics and theme of the book. Book clubs and film clubs are places where the text is a piece of work and the conversation that follows is based on that text. It's a model we'll discuss a lot in the chapter on "Change."

There are sacred texts that can serve the same purpose, sometimes as a backdrop for a broader conversation and sometimes as a frame for the conversation. Think of the Passover Haggadah, which is literally a script to be read over dinner with pauses for conversation. Repetitive and ritualistic, these scripts do more than just give fodder for a conversation; they supply a rhythm and a structure for how to have those conversations.

Scripts are not by nature good or bad. But we can approach

them purposefully and treat them as a means to make that conversation have more form, give it a better feel, or move it forward. Then they become invaluable. Almost every chapter from here on out will work with some different form of script: context will be all about space; constraints will look closely at rules; while change will look at the role of texts, sacred and otherwise, as a structure for cathartic conversations.

While these scripts will be discussed thoroughly and in depth in these chapters, it's important to start "script-spotting" now. When you experience a conversation, spot the scripts. See how they work in action; see whether people are aware of them at all. Take note, and even write about it in your conversation notebook. Even calling out a script has the potential to change a conversation completely.

CHAPTER 4
CONTEXT

The more living patterns there are in a place—a room, a building, or a town—the more it comes to life as an entirety, the more it glows, the more it has that self-maintaining fire, which is the quality without a name.

—*Christopher Alexander*

In an empty warehouse in San Francisco, thirty people were gathered inside a white foam core model. The group was comprised of executives and owners from one of the world's largest hotel chains, a few of their regular customers, and designers. The model was a full-scale replica of a lobby. Its construction in white foam core was cheap and easy to build with, allowing the design team to change the configuration in an instant, moving or removing something from the space in response to feedback.

If the way the reception desk was built didn't allow for an open and informal conversation between guests and hotel staff, it could be changed. If a cozy breakfast seating area was just a bit too cozy, it could be expanded. The space could change based on the conversations happening in it.

This full-scale architectural model had been a dream of mine since I joined IDEO. I'd long been troubled by the difficulty of explaining the language of architecture to clients (as we've already discussed), not to mention drawings and tabletop models of buildings. So my idea was to adopt the prototyping culture of IDEO product design to create full-scale prototypes that let people directly understand what a space felt like because they were actually in that space.

Over the years we became experts at using this full-scale prototyping. We co-built and co-designed hospital corridors and rooms with nurses and doctors to provide spaces that provided intimacy, privacy, and ease of health-care delivery. We once took over a Peruvian bank for days, continuously playing with the configuration of the space in a way that shortened wait times while increasing sociability. At one point, as we worked on the future design of workplace cubicles, we realized that we'd only ever worked in open offices, so we built a "cube farm" in the middle of IDEO's San Francisco office. As a team we all moved into adjacent cubicles, vigilantly observing the ways it affected our interactions, conversations, and collaboration; as it turned out, working in that context significantly changed how we engaged with each other, in many ways for the better.

We were experimenting with context.

Context, as we will explore it in this chapter, is comprised of the spaces we inhabit, the things in those spaces, and the positions we choose to take in that space. It is a mistake to think of context as "just in the background." The context of a conversation can affect the course of a conversation, the feel of it, the outcome; it can even determine what kind of conversations we have. Some of the tools we've explored so far—listening, getting clear on language, establishing principles—are essentially the script of a conversation. Context, space, and the things in that space are the stage.

Sometimes space can be used as a light prompt—for example, facing a first date across a table as opposed to sitting side by side. Sometimes there is a script so hardwired into a room that only very specific conversations can happen in it (as in a courtroom).

The right room shapes conversation. Some spaces inspire creativity and collaboration; others can trigger catastrophic conversations or, as I'll explain later, even trigger memories of previous traumatic experiences that occurred in that space. (Think high school cafeteria!)

However, with forethought, we can choose a context to suit our purpose and exercise creative control of the conversations that we have. Likewise, as we explore this chapter, we'll look at ways that a change of position, or changing what's in a room, can provide cues to guide the kind of conversation you want to make. Taking or reclaiming control of space and position can reset the conversations we have in them.

Purpose-Pick the Space

I proposed to my husband sitting on a wooden pier on a pond in upstate New York. Not surprisingly, people take the place where they propose very seriously; there are even consultants you can hire who will help you find the perfect place to propose and set up the space to ensure the best outcome.

Even if you wouldn't pay someone to help you propose, it is highly unlikely that you would choose the place for a wedding proposal at random. A proposal is a conversation with a desired outcome; a proposal will establish a lifelong memory and where it happened will be a part of that memory. Not all situations are as seriously reliant on setting, but all can benefit from thinking carefully about the places you pick.

For example, some friends of mine recently made a significant move, picking up their teenage son and preteen triplet daughters and relocating to Abu Dhabi to teach on the NYU campus there. They were given a modern apartment with a spacious breakfast bar built into the kitchen. Purely by default and convenience, their evening meals had become a kind of factory assembly line, the four children sitting in a row as meals were delivered by the parents who cooked, served, and ate while standing.

One afternoon we were at lunch, seated around a small round table. They remarked on how open the discussion was, how easy it was to hold one conversation. They were certain it was the round table that facilitated the interaction. By the end of the meal, they had decided to return to their apartment and move dinner from the kitchen bar to a round table in the dining room.

Not long after, I saw them at a gathering and asked how their experiment had gone and received a look of frustration. They explained that they had gone home with the idea of replacing the table, they'd even picked one out, but when they got to their apartment, they realized it could never happen. Their dining room was a long, narrow rectangle, not picked for their purpose.

In the pages that follow, we will look at three elements that can be considered and used as you think about purpose-picking the space: cultural associations, personal association, and the "archetype" effect.

CULTURAL ASSOCIATIONS, ICONIC SPACES

I'll often throw out a simple question at a dinner party, asking people to describe a certain kind of conversation, for instance: "Describe a board meeting." Ninety percent of the time I don't get a description of the conversation at all, rather a description of the spaces where that kind of conversation typically happens. Say "board meeting," and people will likely describe a long mahogany table, leather chairs, and someone in a suit sitting at the head of the table.

Throw out the example of an AA meeting and you'll also get a description of the space: a basement, folding chairs, maybe a folding table with snacks. We have very clear kinds of associations of what kinds of conversation happen in what kinds of spaces. The opposite is obviously true too: when we see spaces, we often imagine the conversations that might happen there.

Think back to the John Dewey Academy. The castle that

houses the school plays a significant role in the ongoing conversations that happen there. First, it has a very specific and remarkably fortunate cultural association: almost every parent and student I spoke to referred to Hogwarts from Harry Potter. So many families have grown up reading the series, and while other schools may feel cold or institutional, Dewey is not just warm but mysterious, even a bit magical.

"Obviously, with this generation we work with a lot of kids who have that connotation," Andrea Lein, the headmaster, told me. "I mean, this could be any kind of boarding school in a castle, right? But they have that Hogwarts connotation, and we're so focused on personal character development that it's a cool, weird coincidence. We have one student now who's unusual because since day one, she's been like, 'I love it here.' She is thrilled to be here. She's like, 'It's so cool. Yeah, I get to live in a castle.'"

The context pervades everything there; it even shifts the language the students use. There, grade levels aren't numeric, or freshmen and seniors. The two levels are "castle-dwellers" and "gatekeepers." Castle-dwellers are younger students still learning the ways of the school and seeking more constant guidance, while the gatekeepers are more senior, more self-sufficient, and more capable of living on their own, at the edge of the property and the rest of the world.

The point is: context permeates everything. So be thoughtful about your context.

PERSONAL ASSOCIATION OR "MNEMONIC" SPACES

My great-grandmother had a swing big enough for two people on her back patio. That same swing had been on the front porch of the farmhouse she had raised her children in. The swing was where you went in the early summer evenings to sit and that swing was where her evening stories were told. Years after my great-grandmother had died, I would find myself sitting on the swing, flush with the warmth and wistfulness brought on by the memory of the conversations we had there.

Mnemonic association is a concept we use when we're trying to memorize something. We'll link a fact to a key word or acronym and so on. When I was a child, I was taught how to eat—or rather how not to eat—an artichoke by our family friend Arthur, who explained not to eat the leaves whole, saying, "Remember, if I eat the leaves, Arty will choke." That was the use of a mnemonic to teach me an important life lesson.

Mnemonic associations are real, and they are often deeply tied to the spaces we inhabit. In recent studies on the science of memory-making, space figures prominently. When an episodic memory of traumatic or joyful events is formed, the brain often uses details of the space we were in to establish that memory. Later, that space can trigger the recovery of that memory. This is why we often ask questions like, "Where were you when the Twin Towers fell?" and it's why we almost always remember. That memory of that powerful event was built in part by observation of the context you were in when it happened.

So, when I talk about "haunted spaces," I'm not speaking about phantoms and creaky doors, rather the real haunting of our personal or "mnemonic" associations. My great-grandmother's swing was haunted not by her spirit but by my memory of her; in this case the association was positive. Later, I'll talk about a bank redesign project where we realized that for many people, a kitchen table has positive cultural associations; people we spoke with had some mnemonic association that was positive. So in that particular case, we had in essence a twofer: good cultural associations and positive mnemonic associations.

No matter how good the cultural associations are, however, they can be completely undone by a negative personal association.

Let me tell you another story about another table. I recently met a family that had lived for years with a deep rift over their daughter's eating disorder. The site of most of the family's arguments—the place where the internal pain manifested—was the dining table. As the daughter grew up and the family worked through their issues, they were able to heal and resume a positive familial dynamic, except when they were reunited at the family dinner table. The table was essentially "haunted" by the conversations that had occurred there before. It was such an impediment to the family dynamic that, at one point, the mother bought a new dining room table and they eventually gave up eating in the dining room altogether.

THE "ARCHETYPE" EFFECT OR EMBEDDED SCRIPTS

There's a book I loved as a young architect, written by Christopher Alexander, called *A Pattern Language*. Alexander was a huge influence on me, and he documents approximately 250 different patterns historically found in space. They range from "a house for two people" to "a beer hall." One of my favorites of his patterns is "alcove seating." An "inglenook" is an example: a small, enclosed alcove with room for two to four people to sit, often built around a hearth. You may never have heard of an inglenook, never been in one, but it's easy to imagine the kind of intimate, warm, and comforting conversations that might happen there.

Alexander argues that these patterns have been embedded in our architecture for thousands of years, maybe as long as we've been building buildings. And we're so familiar with them, they're so embedded in us, that when we enter a space, we naturally know how to behave and live and act inside it. There is, actually, increasing evidence that these "embedded scripts" trigger our brains to process things differently. Whether because of thousands of years of cultural association or some mystery of the brain's mechanics, some spaces will make us think, act, and converse in very different ways.

Think about stairs, for example. The stairs in your apartment building—how you stop to chat on them, or how when you're having a house party, the staircase is almost always the place for the intimate tête-à-tête. Think about large public stairs used for group gatherings, the kind you find in town plazas, off great museums, the Spanish Steps in Rome.

In the pattern "Stairs as Stage," Alexander suggests treating stairs as a room. If you're designing outside stairs, consider them a courtyard and make them wide enough to encourage people to sit and gather on them. Studies show that having conversations on stairs, even just three stairs up, makes us feel more "elevated." There is a kind of psychological trigger built into stairs.

When the IDEO team did the initial design work for the

New School's University Center—which was built to be the university's hub—the whole building was constructed around steps. There were expansive steps, where huge groups could gather for a class, and smaller nooks on stairways that acted like conversational eddies. The large central stairway could host huge town halls of hundreds of people or a casual lunch between friends.

Despite the fact that sitting on stairs feels informal, stairs also imbue spaces with a sense of grandeur and dignity. The setting may be dramatic and awe-inspiring while also being a space that feels approachable and informal, resulting in a positive, creative tension. Sitting on steps is intimate and close, but the vista and openness allow for the mind to be free. In addition, stairs are a place where transitions occur; they invite spontaneity and flexibility.

Conversations on steps can grow and adapt and even pull in a passerby or two, interjecting an entirely different kind of script into the previous one.

Years after the University Center building opened, the stairs continue to be crammed with people engaged in conversation. I did not invent steps, but I did purpose-pick stairs as a way to establish the script of the building. You don't have to be an architect to learn to purpose-pick spaces and spatial scripts to support the kinds of conversations you want to make happen.

A simple way to do this is to jot down five adjectives that describe the qualities of a space. Let's take examples from some of the spaces Alexander uses: a beer hall, a public stairway, and an inglenook.

I'd describe a beer hall as informal, lively, vibrant, active, and comfortable.

The stairs at, say, the Metropolitan Museum are grand, ex-pansive, solid, public, and lively.

The inglenook is closed, warm, safe, intimate, and small.

When you read all five words, they suggest very different spaces. These adjectives also happen to be clues to the conver-sations you can have in these spaces.

Let's say I'm doing an informal check-in with a coworker. I'm looking for an upbeat engagement, a bit of exploration, but I don't want it to get too heavy. It's clear that either the kitchen table or the grand stairway could work for me. The inglenook, if I could even find one, might work but it might be a bit too intimate—maybe I'd choose to have a long conversation about someone's goals and aspirations but not a quick check-in. This might seem obvious, but that's why it's better to take someone out for coffee than to chat in a spare conference room. It's lively, noisy, upbeat. We're all looking for our inglenook.

Want to get more sophisticated? Meet my friend Alex Gal-lafent, who has a background in theater and journalism; he is a fearless designer of dialogue. Once he was asked to design a discussion between business leaders, policy makers, and philan-thropists on the topic of low-wage work in America. He gave a lot of thought to the topic but almost as much consideration to the space where this gathering would be held. The location was to be a renovated monastery, which included a confer-ence center. Though the space had modern features, many ele-ments from the original building remained and were relatively untouched—notably a stone parlor with a massive fireplace and an adjacent open courtyard with a fountain.

Alex chose to move two portions of the conversation out of

the main conference room. We needed to discuss the aspiration of low-wage workers, and the obstacles that stood in their way. That discussion, Alex decided, would be held in the parlor.

The parlor was dark, closed, tight, cold, and austere. It was sort of like a bad version of the inglenook.

The discussion we had in that space was hard. The room was claustrophobic for fifteen people, and the conversation that ensued reflected that atmosphere. The discussion got dark; the political and economic system in this country felt impossibly stacked against the lower class; it felt designed toward exploitation and stagnation; and our conversation ended with all of us wondering, "Can these people even afford to dream?"

We were released into the courtyard, which was soaring, sunlit, green, open, and calm.

There was immediate relief. People remained pensive, but the space inspired expansiveness. There we were asked to discuss what our organizations could do for those workers. When we came back to the conference room, we had both deep empathy for the people we had been discussing and also hope about what we might do.

This piece of the conversation purposely shifted from compression to expansion. The very literal constraints of the first space—its tightness, its darkness—translated into a feeling of oppression and hopelessness. That's what Alex wanted—to create a contrast between present-day challenges and future possibilities. By moving the group from the dark parlor to the airy courtyard, Alex purpose-picked the space for the conversation he wanted to create.

An important thing to remember: Some settings can help cue up a conversation, but they should be supportive players, not the dominant voice. Creative conversations should hold a room, not be dominated by the room itself.

In recent years, some conference organizers have pushed the limits of what a creative space needs to be: office spaces where break rooms have been replaced by ball pits or conference seats suspended ten feet above the ground in order to help participants "get a different perspective." Yes, that might be playing off the inherent effect of elevation, but I'd argue that psychological state is lost in the adrenaline and fear that you may fall. These settings physically manifest a metaphor—playfulness or vantage points—and force rich conversations into a series of one-liners.

Don't get fancy; do get deliberate.

Using Things to "Tune" a Space

While spaces have an enormous impact on the conversations that happen in them, there are many ways to shift the character and quality of the rooms we're in. That's the good news. Often, it's as simple as what's in the room or the way the room is furnished, and even small simple cues can allow you to take control of your context.

Furniture, technology, and objects are tools to help advance, alter, or affect a conversation. As with space, furniture can change the feel of the context you're in and thereby alter a conversation. Furniture carries its own significant associations. As with the AA meeting and the boardroom, the folding chair or mahogany table have as much to do with establishing the context as the church basement or wood-paneled boardroom.

Let's go back to the table for a moment. In 2006 IDEO was hired by a European bank to look at how to engage bank customers and to build trust between them and the highly trained financial advisers on staff. This work was specifically focused in Eastern Europe—the banks in this part of the world had collapsed recently, and smart citizens felt they knew how best to manage their money, hiding cash under mattresses and taking only informal advice of family and friends. As the bank built new branches, they put their financial advisers in private offices at impressive desks. Customers would file by to cash their checks, ignore the offices, and take that cash home.

We started by going into people's homes to spend time with families and talk about the financial decisions that they made. We sat with people at their kitchen tables. We'd ask how they made financial decisions and who gave them advice; in most cases it was family and friends. When we asked where they had those conversations, it was almost always at the very place we were sitting then: the kitchen table—often over vodka.

The team made a simple one-to-one translation, without the vodka. We built a new bank branch replacing the polished wood desks and glass walls of the office with a set of small "kitchen tables" where the offices used to be. When a bank employee offered financial advice, now gesturing to the kitchen table, there was no hesitation. Bank customers saw the tables and would take a seat. The space we designed carried just enough of the positive cultural associations of the kitchen table to make the conversation feel more familiar and approachable.

Kitchen tables are, by nature, intimate things; they are associated with family rather than guests, domesticity rather than entertaining, informality rather than formality. They even subtly connect with new beginnings—it's where we often eat breakfast rather than dinner, and our bodies are most primed for optimism in the morning. Rabbi Elliot Cosgrove once said of Golda Meir that "she used her kitchen wisely," an Israeli saying. She would often invite visiting dignitaries and heads of state into her kitchen for important conversations.

Architects and interior designers seemed to discover this cultural association to the kitchen table in the early 2000s as they were being asked to build a new generation of work spaces. Right now, there are probably more kitchen tables in Silicon Valley office spaces than there are in Silicon Valley homes. This purposeful spotting and adaptation of this cultural association of informal domesticity and comfortable conversations was an aspiration for these workplaces.

Another time, I was asked to redesign a board meeting. The chair of the board wanted the meeting to feel more retreat-like and relaxed. The space I was given was the same boardroom we always met in, and there was nothing retreat-like about it.

Given the limited time and no resources, I was forced to do a simple reset of the space I had.

I removed what had been a giant U-shaped table and shifted the seating to many small round tables. It was a basic, last-minute move, the only move at my disposal. But the instinct was inspired by the cultural associations of a round table.

That said, it was a complete surprise to many. As people entered the room, nobody quite knew what to do; this just wasn't the way a boardroom looked. It wasn't until the chair of the board walked in and exclaimed, "Lunchroom seating!" that people knew the tables were for them. That personal mnemonic association was not the connotation I had expected, but to my surprise—given my experience with lunchroom conversations—it served us well. The conversation was lively, people bonded, and good kinds of cliques were formed. When we took time for breaks, the board members were reluctant to leave "their seats" at "their tables." What I thought would be a minor shift turned out to be a complete reimagining of the social setting.

There are very simple ways to take control of your context; some edits, some additions, and the board meeting became a board retreat.

TAKE CONTROL OF YOUR CONTEXT: EDIT OR ADD

There are other kinds of "things" that affect context that can be subtler than furniture but no less impactful; I think of them as props. Props in plays are the objects on the stage. Stages are small and sets are not reproductions of the real world, so if a prop is onstage it has to advance the action or give insight into the characters' personality or psychology. That's exactly the role we want props to play in creative conversation.

The things—or props—we purposefully place into the context of a conversation should do one of two things: reveal something hidden or propel things forward.

TAKE IT AWAY

Always edit first. Get things out of the room. It's a basic but important act of creative control. Why? Because there are already props in place, just not the good kind.

I hope it's self-evident, but phones are not a prop at all. They do not reveal your emotion to the group in any good way, and they do not propel collective conversation. I guess they might reveal that you're bored, they can help propel you into a world of your own, but that is not the kind of props we're looking for.

To be blunt, most technology is a bad prop. If there's a conferencing device or speakerphone in the room, everyone still looks at the device instead of looking at each other. We still don't know how to turn on the microphone, mute, or un-mute. Too many important conversations require equally important participants to crawl under the table to make things work.

Make a clean start. Get Marie Kondo on your conversation—whatever isn't bringing conversational joy goes out the door.

Look around the rooms you meet in and ask yourself what doesn't add to the conversation. It's likely a lot, but then really ask yourself what might hold you back. Any hindrances you can remove, remove them. Be careful of finger spinners and fidget toys. Have Post-its and pens, but only when you want to use them.

In particular look for things that are specters of the kinds of conversations you might not want to have. A meeting room with a podium that no one will ever stand at—that's a figure in the shadows. Somebody else's whiteboard drawing means somebody else's conversations are as important as yours.

While there is a lot of controversy about the idea of "clean desk" policies in the workplace, studies do link unwanted clutter in the workplace to feelings of "emotional exhaustion" and decision fatigue, and this is clearly not an association you want to bring into any creative conversation. Messy desk, fine—messy meeting space, not so much.

Wipe down the whiteboard, that ghost of conversations past; make sure there are not tons of empty seats, which make a space forlorn; gather and put away anything that's on a table, extraneous Post-its, coffee cups, and of course phones. Do the same at home: clear the clutter from a dining table and set the table together. Do not have dinner with your bills and unopened mail; instead choose your dinner partner—even if it's just you—instead.

It's your conversation. Take care to unclutter it.

NOW ADD

At IDEO there has always been a saying: "Never show up to a meeting without a prototype." This advice came out of product design, where a very rough version of the thing you're making can clarify more for a client than thousands of words. Product prototypes stimulate and focus the conversation—which is why I was so intent on using spatial prototypes as we built the space practice at IDEO.

Prototypes work well for design conversations but bringing something real into the room—a prop—can catalyze almost any conversation. The props to bring to a conversation should be chosen to help reveal something that might otherwise be hidden—emotions, for instance.

Not long after the 2016 elections, we hosted a set of un-moderated conversations in Washington, DC. The discussions were between very different people—educators, journalists, government workers. Many at the tables were from mixed political backgrounds, and it was a moment of heightened sensitivity.

These were uneasy conversations that had the potential to become uncomfortable, even contentious. We needed something that could allow people to express disagreement without all-out conflict.

We thought carefully about context in the space we chose. It was a dinnertime conversation. The space was in a lively restaurant, where some form of civility had to be maintained. The tables were round. We wanted a conversation that was synthetic and healing, not fractious. We'd thought out so many of the context elements—the space, the furniture, and the position. But there was something else we needed . . . something that could help propel the conversation forward if it got stuck. We wanted a way for deeper, maybe even darker, more difficult feelings to come forward.

So we added a prop.

Njoki Gitahi, a designer who has a knack for the elegant and beautiful, designed a simple prop that I still carry with me today. It was a two-sided, illustrated card. One side had a glowing bright star, the other a hooded dark shadow. Bright Star and Black Hole.

The card sat to the side of the silverware and we suggested that people participating in the discussion hold one side of the card up, Black Hole or Bright Star, depending on how they were feeling about the topic being discussed. The prop allowed everyone to talk and, at the same time, express concern or hope. The card allowed for a conversation with momentum and engagement without letting any single emotion take the forefront; it was additive, not interruptive.

I had expected people to lift their cards based on what we were discussing. What I hadn't expected was that whoever was speaking would tune themselves—just a bit—to the emotion being displayed around the table. There was a kind of live editing that the card enabled throughout the discussion.

And then, at one point, as someone talked about her daughter, everyone lifted the card, Bright Star face forward.

It turned out that almost everyone at the table had a daughter. People started to reveal themselves. Some at the table hadn't attended the Women's March with their daughters; they fervently believed in the causes being represented, but also believed it interfered with their journalistic integrity. Others who were quite conservative had issues with abortion, for instance, but had attended the march because it felt too momentous to keep their girls from going.

Despite the differences in the attendees, the conversation ended up being a deep and exploratory discussion of girls, from toddlers to teens, how they develop, and the risks they take. The fact that so many of the participants were deeply committed to the future of girls, their girls, was only revealed by the short flash of a bright star.

People left with new empathy and political beliefs intact. The prop revealed emotions and a conversational path with the simplest of gestures.

This is what I hope for when I play with context. Without the right context, we would have never discovered the commonality that everyone at the table shared, and that discovery was what bonded them. A small, thoughtful, and revealing prop can be especially useful in moments where conversations are hard to start, or in conversations that are difficult to stall. Everyone took their prop home with them that night. Mine is pinned above my desk right now as I work, Bright Star side facing me, resetting my context just enough to keep me going.

Take a Position, Literally

Position—literally how and why we arrange our bodies—is part of context too. Take, for example, one of our most common conversational contexts: sitting together in a car. Planned Parenthood actually recommends that a car ride is the best time to have open conversations with your children about sex. The position—side by side, or front seat, back seat—is less challenging, the body language is nonconfrontational. No eye contact makes hard conversations easier or at least lets you hide how hard they are.

If you've ever been on a long car ride with a friend, you may have experienced the Planned Parenthood position in practice. You may not have talked openly about sex, but chances are you did talk more openly in general. Side by side alleviates some of the potential for conflict. You can't see your companion's facial expressions head-on, and the slight distraction of driving allows the mind the bit of escape it needs when things get awkward. Listening becomes slightly meditative. Buddy movies are often road movies; Thelma and Louise wouldn't have become friends sitting in a cubicle.

Some contexts force us into position—the car, public steps, or round tables, for example. Other contexts can be shifted and tuned by simply changing the position we're in. Taking position seriously is the best way to alter an otherwise uncooperative context.

We learn from a very early age that where and how you sit matters. Positions, and the power they have, are something we intuitively grasp but don't do much with. The positions we feel comfortable taking are often dictated by convention, etiquette, or the existing structures and spaces. Once you start to consider how people are positioned in a conversation, you realize that as a society we have become victim to the tyranny of the table.

Increasing research in cognitive science accumulates evidence that our bodies and our minds are deeply in sync. Not only does what we think have an effect on how we feel physically, but the research confirms that how our body feels has an effect on our emotional outlook as well. This notion of "embodied cognition"—the mind/body interplay—suggests that small things like forcing a smile might actually make us feel happier or, as mentioned earlier, elevating the body on a few steps might make us in turn feel more hopeful.

Your body can change your mind. How you sit or stand in relation to each other has an undeniable impact on how a conversation happens. What people are willing to say, even the outcomes of a conversation, can be shifted by simply shifting position. The conventions around the positions we take can be changed. Purposeful positioning will be surprising, yes, but it's also surprisingly welcomed.

There is a perfect position for every conversation you want to have—you just have to find it. Pay close attention to what your body feels or the personal mnemonic associations a position brings to mind. Let's start with the simplest and most powerful position of all: the circle.

THE NOT SO SECRET POWER OF A CIRCLE

"What is it with circles?"

I was chatting with Keri Putnam, the executive director of the Sundance Institute, who had just spent the day reviewing old footage and photographs of Sundance in its early days and had been seeing a lot of circles.

The land where the Sundance Institute holds its artist labs was purchased by Robert Redford after he had filmed the movie *Butch Cassidy and the Sundance Kid* there. He started using the property for filmmaking retreats, and because the land had originally been settled by Native Americans, he built Native American rituals into the lab practices.

When Keri asked the question, she was referring to those rituals, but also the fact that a lot of the institute's work happens in circles. Script readings are in circles, critiques are in circles, opening and closing ceremonies are in circles.

Standing or sitting in a circle feels slightly awkward. Circles feel both natural and yet somewhat outside of the norm. In a circle, everyone is equally visible; circles without tables in them ask the people in the circle to fill the void.

The psychologist Carl Jung said that circles "represent the wholeness of the psychic ground or, to put it in mythic terms, the divinity incarnate in man." Circles are closely related to spiritual power, religion, and ritual. Many tribal cultures around the world meet or practice spiritual rituals in circles, women's circles are a practice for spiritual healing, and evangelical Christians use prayer circles. The sun dance itself, which the film institute and festival take its name from, was a circular ritual often representing the cycle of the year.

There may be spiritual power in circles, but today there may be a simpler explanation for their power: we live in squares. We inhabit square or rectangular rooms in square or rectangular buildings, and we sit at rectangular tables. When we sit or stand in a circle, we are rebelling against our most common understanding of the way spaces are built and that our daily lives play out. When we sit and converse in a circle, we're completely resetting the conversation structures we know.

When the space and setting are against you, sitting in a circle is a good first step.

WHAT IF WE RECLINE?

We rarely find ourselves in formal conversation in recline, but that's because being in recline triggers informality. That informal position, however, has played a key part in important conversations throughout history.

Over the years, I've had the opportunity to work with George Papandreou, the former prime minister of Greece. In many ways I think of him as a tutor who has offered unique insight into dialogue and how it happens. Part of his knowledge comes from his firsthand experience of government in crisis, but it's his knowledge of Greek history—thousands of years of thinking about how democratic dialogue happens—that I find uniquely inspiring.

Every year George holds a gathering for a couple of days on a different Greek island. The topic is almost always focused on the heady topic of world affairs. The event itself, however, is sprawling and informal. Even when conversations do happen in formal settings, it's highly likely that toddlers are playing hide-and-seek under the table; lunches go long, and participants linger over wine. Economists, entrepreneurs, politicians, and their husbands, wives, children, and grandchildren migrate from the conference room to the dining table, where the real conversations happen. Days often end with conversations continuing while participants stand waist-high in the Mediterranean; dinners often end with dancing.

These conferences are unlike any other I've ever attended, yet they are based in part on a three-thousand-year-old idea of how a creative conversation should happen: the Greek symposium.

According to George, symposia were traditional forums to discuss philosophical and artistic issues of the day. Greek philosophers, poets, and politicians of all classes—though all male—were invited. These were moments to discuss important topics, but they were equally important for forging bonds between the participants, many of whom were seen as important players in the Greek political infrastructure, the polis.

If you ever see a representation of the symposium, often depicted on ancient Greek pottery, the most distinctive thing about them was that the entire conversation happened in re-cline. Chaises and benches were placed around the room so that participants could see each other, while in recline. The conversation could be energetic, long, wandering on complex topics, and they could last for hours, even days. But it was a bit hard for outright hostility; in fact, the conversation was more likely to wade off into gossip or personal advice than heated argument.

The original symposium was held in rooms specifically for this kind of conversation. The discussion was frequently in-terrupted by poetry, singing, and other musical performances. Elaborate meals were served, and wine was poured liberally and strategically. The word *symposium* itself comes from the term *sympa*, the word for the wine pitcher. The person who poured the wine—also called the Sympa—kept an eye out for partic-ipants who needed a bit more lubrication to open up or oth-ers who, with just one more glass of wine, might be too drunk to string words together at all. The Sympa was an earlier and much more interesting form of moderator.

In Nathan Kravis's book *On the Couch* he points out that throughout history reclining has been associated with social conversations and reflective storytelling. It's this association between internal exploration and public sharing that, he be-lieves, led Freud to adopt the reclining position as a part of psychoanalytic practice.

Reclining, it turns out, might be the perfect position to add to creative conversations. If it triggers emotional openness, has associations with a luxurious attitude toward time, and patience and openness between participants, then shouldn't it be in our creative mindset as we think of ways to control a conversation?

STAND UP!

Standing meetings have gotten sort of a bad reputation. Associated with technology start-ups and programming mindsets, they're currently intertangled with tech culture—for good and for bad. But, remember, standing has been around for a while.

Here are the benefits of standing: it makes you more alert, it raises energy, it helps you focus and shed bad postures, it makes weird body language dissipate, and all the props we have, good and bad, must go by the wayside. When it developed as a practice in tech culture, the stand-up was appropriated from pre-play team huddles, in which athletes gather to help build energy. It works.

When I was doing the scenography work with the Ritz-Carlton, I got to attend a lot of Ritz-Carlton morning lineups. The morning lineup is a ten-minute gathering of staff on a property or in a corporate office. The lineup can happen in a lobby, a meeting room, or a hallway. The lineup happens precisely at 9:00 a.m. They're hosted by a rotating volunteer, and every meeting is a conversation on one topic of importance, some operational news. They typically culminate with a brief discussion of one of the organization's four key principles. In my experience, everyone on the staff leaves that lineup more energized and inspired.

Here's the most important thing about stand-ups: They're a chance to see and connect to people in a genuine way without the trappings of a typical meeting or conversation. A chance to connect to our values as a collective. Please do make sure to stand up, but also please make sure to consider what it is you're standing for.

GET GROUNDED

While you might not have learned everything in kindergarten, there are some things that linger from when you were five.

Sitting cross-legged on the ground is something we have undeniably good associations with. It could be the memory of story time in the library, picnics with family, or simple classroom games. Can you think of a more liberating moment than when the formal structure of classroom in your teens or twenties was broken by a surprising spring day and a teacher who agreed to hold class outside? You may not remember what was discussed, but you likely remember the positive impression of the moment.

In 2012 I worked with future senator Elizabeth Warren and her staff as they started to establish the engagement strategy of the Consumer Financial Protection Bureau (CFPB). At the time, Elizabeth Warren was an outspoken Harvard professor who had written a significant book on financial inequity in America. The CFPB, which was built in 2011 in response to the 2007–8 financial crisis, came together fast, in offices that sprawled over a building close to the White House. There were meeting rooms, tables, whiteboards, but the offices were missing one thing: chairs. There were plenty of places to meet, but a significant lack of chairs.

We would scatter on the floor of conference rooms, and it was impossible to reproduce the rigid formality of a typical government conference table, where senior staff sit at the table and junior staff sit in rows and rows behind. In these early group meetings, we would sit cross-legged, all mixed up, wherever we could find a spot, and it was often hard to locate senior staff or differentiate them from the interns.

The CFPB then, and in the years that followed, was one of the more collaborative and open work cultures I've encountered. No one was afraid to speak, no one was afraid to ask hard—or for that matter, dumb—questions. Everyone participated, and while I know leadership and mission had a role in shaping that culture, I do believe that part of that collaborative culture was born from the fact that, at least for a couple months, their senior leadership and staff were forced to have their most important and strategic conversations sitting cross-legged on the floor.

When we did finally move to more formal conference rooms, hierarchy dictated where people sat, but the dialogue continued to engage anyone, from anywhere in the room. There was a new position in place, but the behavior established on the floor persisted.

Don't take your position for granted. Make seating charts, get low, get everyone to stand, but, whatever you do, take control of position, don't let it control you. Reflect on the conversations you have, how they feel, and the position you're in. They are all connected. Start to notice where people sit and how conversations feel. When everything else cannot be fixed, you may still be able to change position. You may not be able to choose the space you're in, but taking a different position in that space can retune that space significantly.

Don't Waste Space

Just as you wouldn't want to live your life in the same room, having all your conversations around a conference room table entangled in phone wires and bedecked with laptops seriously limits the range of emotion and engagement you can expect from the discussions you have.

That's why exploring your context can be so endlessly rewarding.

Get good at understanding how a space feels, what it means. Pick the space for the conversation you want—it becomes a whole new way of exploring the world. Don't be afraid to just get up and leave a space if it's not working. Find somewhere else, more fitting.

Likewise, become attentive to subtle things like props; they can open up whole new ways to have a conversation or enable conversations you didn't think you could have at all.

And when all else fails, just change your position. Establishing the right energy through the right position can happen anywhere and anytime in a conversation.

There's a universe of new creative energy to be released by playing with context.

That said, if we'd had class every day outside on the lawn, eventually the position and the setting would feel less and less special. Overusing any of these tools—spaces, position, or props—can rob contexts of the associations that give them power.

Save up on the contexts that are truly unique and use them when you're facing a conversation that matters most. Use the corner coffee shop all you want but keep some of the more extreme spaces in reserve. After all, special or particularly difficult kinds of conversations deserve once-in-a-lifetime kinds of spaces—reserve the monastery courtyard for the conversation that really matters.

Conversation Break: Peaceful Interruption

When I was first asked to conduct onstage interviews with experts and other notable people, I reached out to an expert. Linda Tischler, who was then the design editor for *Fast Company*, had done more creativity-centered "onstage" interviews than anyone I knew. She agreed to meet up and give me a couple of tips she'd learned. She gave invaluable advice and as we were wrapping up, she stopped and said:

"Oh, most important, learn to interrupt people gracefully when they won't stop talking."

"Right, what have you learned that works best in that situation?" I asked.

"I never have" was her answer.

That short exchange really stuck. There must be some good way to interrupt people when they dominate a conversation.

Ironically, the very word *interruption* is somewhat problematic, as it has jolting and negative connotations. If you search for synonyms you will discover only negatives, things like *break in, interfere, barge in on,* even *heckle.* Interrupting someone—even when they dominate—just feels kind of rude.

Peaceful—and purposeful—interruption, however, can have a powerful impact on the practice of dialogue. We've talked about a few versions of peaceful interruption already, when we explore things like shifting the rules or observing a minute of silence, and it's a big part of the change chapter. As a practice, it's worthwhile observing where and when peaceful interruption happens and begin to take note.

Reflect on the kinds of situations where peaceful interruption is merited and needed. The first and most obvious is the example I've already cited where someone (or even a small but vocal cohort) is running on or dominating a conversation accidentally or on purpose. Interruption is necessary to allow new voices into a conversation. Another moment that warrants a peaceful interruption is when a conversation is clearly falling apart or seems to be heading into a downward spiral, in essence failing. Here, an interruption can revive a conversation before it fails completely.

In a conversation I had with Lisa Kron, who won a Tony for writing the musical *Fun Home,* we touched briefly on the idea of interruption in theater. One of her plays, *Well,* is essentially a one-woman monologue that is continually interrupted by an actress playing her mother who is supposed to just watch but can't help interrupting. Kron talked about interruption in theater as a "purposeful change of energy." That's the intention behind thinking about interruption and change. With peaceful interruption the point is to purposefully change the energy and the point is that that energy should be well intentioned, peaceful.

The peaceful—and purposeful—interruption that we learn from rituals can have a powerful impact on the practice of dialogue. In my observations, there are some really ingenious ways to create a peaceful interruption. Here are three that I've observed that range from the simple to the spectacular.

1. SILENCE

The natural inclination for fast decision-making is exactly the reason why we need to set rules to slow it down. The director Philip Gröning had heard about a brotherhood of Carthusian monks in the Swiss Alps. These monks were unique now— though not unique in history—for their adherence to a vow of silence. Many of the monks had lived at the same monastery for much of their adult lives, where the rules of the order require that they only speak to each other once a week; the rest of their days are spent in silence. The filming took months as it followed the brotherhood for a complete year. Gröning was able to make a remarkable nearly silent film that chronicled the unique life of this monastic order. *Into Great Silence* is visually beautiful and captures the world of silence and the spirituality of the brotherhood in a unique and vivid way.

What is most telling about this order is not so much in the making of the film but in the process it took to get the film made. The director put in a formal request to the brotherhood to make the documentary and they said they would consider it and connect back. He was delighted when they agreed to his request, even though they "got back to him" sixteen years later.

That may be a bit slow, but it reveals the idea that one of the simplest ways to set rules for slowness is to build in small amounts of silence.

Asking people to slow down decision-making is hard, setting rules that put silence into decision-making is relatively easy, just a small amount of silence can significantly slow conversation down, and seconds of silence can shift the decision-making of a group. Before making a decision or trying to come to consensus, consider pausing for a moment of silence, just a minute.

Established silence is so rare in conversation that it doesn't take much to see change. When John Cage premiered his still controversial *4'33"* seventy years ago, audiences walked out halfway; the four and a half minutes of silence was just too uncomfortable. In groups we typically reserve silence as a way to honor someone's loss or to calm children, not to alter the direction of a conversation. For some this will be comfortable; for others used to speaking it can be unbearably awkward, which is a good thing.

Enough said, take a moment.

2. ASK OR ASSESS

The easiest way to peacefully interrupt is to ask a question. This works well in situations where one person is dominating. A question flatters, and it allows you to express interest in what's being said, while still interrupting the flow. Try asking, "Can you give an example?" It then allows you to ask others if they've shared similar experiences, which shifts from the singular to the group.

When things really seem to be going awry, ask for an assessment. I have a friend who described being in a conversation about strategy at his workplace: Things seemed to be getting fuzzy and unclear—it felt like the conversation was spiraling away from them—and then someone in the room asked the question, "Wait, let's stop and ask, 'What are we talking about?'" Their answers revealed that indeed they had all been talking about different things. After that, they were able to reset and all talk about one thing.

3. SING OUT

Interrupting someone can feel awkward and uncomfortable; interrupting a whole bunch of people is deeply intimidating. But when it's done and done well it can be revolutionary.

Amelia Winger-Bearskin is half Native American and half Jewish. She was raised outside of Rochester by her father who was a businessman at Kodak and her mother who was the official storyteller of her tribe. Trained as an engineer, Amelia is part experimental storyteller and part director of a tech consultancy in New York. She's also an opera singer.

I was once in an all-day meeting with Amelia when we hit that midafternoon moment where so many well-intentioned conversations go awry. People were tired, the room was claustrophobic, and we'd ended up in a deadlock, uncertain how to proceed.

But then Amelia raised her hand. She seemed diminutive in the middle of this conference room—young, pale, dark-haired, almost waif-like. She asked if she could sing to us.

There is a light
it's going to go out
It's the moon tonight
it's going to go out
I sing this song, my baby boy
There's a light
there's a light
and it's going to go out for you for me tonight.
There is a light that shines so bright
It's you, it's the light and it shines tonight
I sing this song, my baby boy
There is a light
there's a light it will never go out for me for you tonight.

Her voice was so clear and strong, her presence completely took over the room. The song was a lullaby she had written for her son, but in the context of this conversation, it served as a reminder that time was short and not to be squandered.

In the moments that followed this interruption, we agreed to restructure the rest of the day together. Amelia had unlocked the desires that ran under the surface of everyone in the room, and she had done so in a singular and spectacular way. We all remember the moment and the aftermath, but to this day it's hard to remember why we had gone awry in the first place.

The introduction of music not only provides peaceful interruption but it tells us something about the people or the person that we couldn't learn just through words. We often see music used at special moments; think, for instance, about how music is often woven into a wedding ceremony or a funeral.

I've been in many meetings where music is played at interludes in a conversation, and once met a successful media executive who describes her voice as terrible yet starts her meetings with a song she sings while reading the lyrics off her cell phone. Musical interludes reset neural pathways in ways similar to taking a moment of silence.

CHAPTER 5

CONSTRAINTS

> If people know the rules, and are sensitized
> by art, humor, and creativity, they are much
> more likely to accept change.
>
> —*Antanas Mockus*

Some people think that IDEO invented brainstorming. But that's not the case. Brainstorming came out of the deep frustration of an advertising executive named Alex Osborn. This was in the 1930s, and Osborn's team kept coming up with ideas that he thought were too limited and too tame. So he developed the notion of a group session devoted solely to idea generation. He originally called it "organized ideation." It might seem ironic, but in order to get his teams to open up, to enjoy and celebrate ideas, he established a very strict set of constraints.

Osborn ended up writing extensively about creativity and was one of the first people to codify a methodology behind creativity and design. His original four rules of brainstorming and the thinking behind them remain a fantastic illustration of why constraints foster creativity and collaboration:

1. Reach for quantity.
2. "Freewheeling" is welcomed.
3. Criticism is ruled out.
4. Combination and improvement are sought.

Now, look at Osborn's description of "criticism is ruled out":

"Adverse judgement of ideas must be withheld until later. Allowing yourself to be critical at the same time you are being creative is like trying to get hot and cold water from one faucet at the same time. Ideas aren't hot enough; judgement isn't cold enough—all you get is lukewarm thinking. We reserve criticism for a later screening session."

Brainstorms, after all, are not meant to give you the idea; they are meant to inspire many ideas. You have to strip judgment away so that people don't feel strange throwing out wild or freewheeling suggestions. And then look at the last rule: "Combination and improvement are sought." In other words, build on each other's ideas. His goal was to identify good ideas and make them better. That's why that particular constraint is so essential. It made sure participants stayed inside one conversation; they needed to listen to the ideas being suggested, push them further, and continually improve them.

In his writing on brainstorming, Osborn also teases the idea that in a later "session" the rules will change, and critique will be allowed. This is important to note as we look at constraints: different actions, goals, and activities require different sets of constraints. As we explore the idea of constraints in this chapter, we will look at how to create constraints, but also when and where we may have to shift those constraints or "change the rules" to get new kinds of outcomes.

When you talk to any designer, they will inevitably extol the virtues of constraints. In a world that celebrates "out-of-the-box thinking," the creative practice is often easier to navigate when there is a box to start with. Constraints can establish the rhythm and pace of a conversation; they can allow for ways to interrupt when things go awry; they also can allow you to shift gears when the goals of that conversation change. The right constraints can make the creative difference in the conversations we have. Constraints create.

Get Clear on Constraints

Eddie Shiomi, my friend who designs leadership training programs, thinks a lot about constraints. He likens trying to navigate a conversation without rules to trying to keep your balance on a subway train where there are no handles. "You keep reaching in different directions but there's nothing to grab onto."

Throughout my research for this book, one of the most frequent questions I've received is: "What rules do you believe in?" The questioner may be thinking of *Robert's Rules of Order*, most often used in boardrooms, government organizations, and other formal settings, or the Socratic method, often used in professional schools, or the rules used in competitive debate teams. My answer tends to be "all of them." I'm basically "rule-curious."

Here's my reasoning: if rules are one of the ways to constrain a conversation—for the better—any of these rule sets and more can be appropriate. The question for me is always: What rules are best for the goals and tone of the conversation, and how were the rules put into place? That last question is really the important one, as all too often we follow rules without knowing their origins.

Without clarity—to go back to one of my earlier tenets of good conversations—it's hard to find the right balance between playfulness and progress. And that's where constraints can be helpful, but only if you know why they are being instituted in the first place.

Build Constraints Together

Here's another vital possibility: build the constraints together. This is such a valuable practice, because collective agreement on constraints does more than establish order—it establishes community. Grade school teachers all over America are getting pretty good at this, using an approach often referred to as the "responsive classroom."

At the beginning of the academic year, the responsive classroom model asks students and teachers, first, to collectively identify their hopes and dreams for the year. Then they gradually home in on a set of rules that will help students fulfill those hopes and dreams—rules they will be guided by throughout the year that are designed to help them achieve their goals.

These classrooms and schools post the rules on the wall, in an almost mural format, as a means of reminding the community of the rules they themselves established.

There is something so essentially optimistic about the idea that rules are there to help them fulfill their aspirations. That's why their rules are reframed as positive action. For example, instead of saying, "Don't say mean things," the rule should be, "Speak kindly." When you shift from negative to positive—"Move safely," instead of, "Don't run," for example—it changes the role of rules. These positive rules help you understand the feeling and community you aspire for. In one school, the first collective rule they set was, "Enjoy!" My favorite rule ever.

Some Constraints for Constraints

So, let's adapt this for our work on constraints.

(Even calling them constraints, to my mind, is taking a page from the responsive classroom practice. Constraints are positive things, whereas rules have a negative connotation. Rules scare us. Constraints free us. Rules restrict. Constraints liberate.)

So, first, establish the goals and the tone for the conversation. Together, tailor the constraints to best suit that goal. And get serious: Write them out. Display them. Don't forget them. The only thing worse than a conversation with no constraints is one where there are constraints and yet they're constantly broken or ignored.

I realize that adding constraints to a conversation can feel fairly intimidating. That's why I want to offer four constraints about constraints:

1. BE SPECIFIC: Ambiguous constraints are essentially worthless. If it needs to be interpreted, then it's probably not a good rule.

A constraint should be as short as it can be, and it should—when it can—tell you exactly what it is it wants you to do. There is no good constraint that requires people to stop and think about whether or how it should be used in a conversation.

2. BE POSITIVE: Again, this goes back to the responsive classroom practice, and it's really stuck with me. We're so used to rules telling us what not to do, it's one of the reasons we may initially reject the idea of rules being placed in a conversation. So make constraints that tell you what to do and who you aspire to be. No constraint should be complex enough or so restrictive that you have to overthink the ability to have a conversation. Making conversation is our goal, not navigating it.

3. BE SURPRISING: A wild-card constraint is what tips participants to the idea that the conversation is in fact a creative one. As you look through the conversational formats discussed in this chapter and in this book, you'll notice that many of them have at least one "out there" constraint. "Remain silent." "Move toward the people you agree with." "Go for quantity." These surprising constraints are often the ones that completely redefine a conversation.

4. BE BRIEF: I'd suggest four at maximum. Four is already a lot for a group to take in and keep in mind. More important, once you go to five or more constraints, you're asking people to learn a system, which is really different from learning the guidelines for how a conversation is run. I attend many meetings that are run by "Robert's Rules," and I find them to be fairly oppressive conversations. There are so many rules, it's easy to get caught up in figuring out the rules rather than grappling with the content of the conversation you intend to be crafting. You're not making conversation; you're instead just intent on following the rules of conduct.

In what follows next, we'll look at three categories of constraints and what they allow us to do: constraints about time and the ways they make us more productive and propel a conversation forward; constraints that make things fairer and allow for more open participation; and, finally, constraints that allow us to critique and push ideas forward.

Remember, you don't need to live in constraints forever; you can and should be rewriting them. Don't get caught up so much with drafting a constraint that you don't get to see it in action; it's only by working with it in a conversation that you understand whether or not it will work.

Time Constraints: Fast, Slow, and Stop

There is no simpler way to influence the tone and tenor of a conversation, the quality of the thinking, and the kind of outcome than setting constraints about time. That's what an agenda does. It is in essence a set of constraints about time and how that time is used.

Agendas tell us when we can speak and when we can't. They suggest what kinds of things need to happen in what kinds of moments and how much or little time we have to make those things happen. They can control the speed of decision-making and the deliberateness of discussion. As you plan a creative conversation, treat an agenda as a set of constraints. It's one of the most important creative differences we can make.

Think about a conference you've attended, a public forum, a professional development conference, or something else altogether. Conferences are an extreme form of conversation and in that way, they're governed by an extreme form of agenda.

Most conferences strive for a measured approach to conversation: Four forty-five-minute sessions in the morning, two ninety-minute "breakouts" in the afternoon. The four morning sessions will be listening to people onstage and are comprised of a panel, or at the very least the morning will end with one. The afternoon sessions, ironically called "breakouts," are where you may get to be more interactive; maybe there's an activity or a group discussion. I'm guessing you've been to a conference like this before. In fact, I'm guessing you've been to a conference like this many times before.

Then there are the conference disruptors—TED being the most famous. One of TED's great innovations was to completely break the rhythm of a typical conference. People were required to put content into tight time frames, time limits that felt almost impossible to get their content into. If you give a TED Talk, eighteen minutes is the longest slot any speaker will have. Love TED or hate it, TED created a completely new formula and pace for a conference, and TED Talks were an innovation in content delivery, inspiring ideas in their most essential form.

If you're not fond of the format, it's likely because you've experienced a bad version of it. We've been so starved for a creative difference in the conference space that TED-like formats have become a seemingly easy antidote. So now, when you go to a conference, you may get a morning of eight or ten eighteen-minute sessions instead of the four forty-five-minute sessions we used to have.

When we set agendas for a conversation or a meeting, we will often strive for the same kind of pattern-making. We'll try to build a timing and format that feels measured, logical, and fair. That's a huge mistake.

After all, the worst enemy of a well-paced and creative conversation is cramming too much into a discussion. We desperately want to get through the uncertainty associated with open-ended discussions and get to some kind of resolution.

When we're making conversation, on the other hand, we should establish a good rhythm, but not necessarily a steady one. A creative conversation should allow for wandering at the right moments, but be rigorous at others; the pace should change, and the rhythm should be syncopated. A creative conversation should be encouraged to move fast at times, deliberative at others, and stop completely when necessary.

After all, different moments, different activities, and different content all require different pacing.

SPEED UP

If we return to the opening example of brainstorming, we can see the value of speeding up some parts of the meeting.

Speeding up is similar to the stand-up meeting we discussed earlier in the book. Going fast excites body and mind while it discourages overthinking. This is why people often set constraints that encourage speed in idea-generation mode:

"Let's get one hundred ideas out in the next fifteen minutes." That's a fine place to think fast, but speed has equally useful applications to topics where we tend toward slow. A lot of good can come from unearthing problems fast but solving them slow.

I was asked to kick off a strategic planning session for the board of a New York art museum. They wanted the board to reflect and gain some consensus on the most pressing issues that the institution was facing. I was offered as much time as I wanted, but opted for speed and chose to use only the last seven minutes of the meeting.

As the meeting was ending, dusk fell over the New York skyline, and wine was about to be served, so I asked the group to pair up with those sitting next to them and take five minutes to identify the three biggest problems the institution faced and the one thing they thought could fix it. There was shock, even panic, on their faces, but given the short time frame, they had no choice but to tackle that list.

Don't be afraid to use fast methods for the places where we tend to wallow.

More important, speed here works just like it does in ideation: less time means less self-censorship. Afterward, the conversation was buzzy, lively—it showed that the group was as inspired and excited by the issues they faced as if they had invented one hundred solutions.

SLOW DOWN: SMART STOPS

Enforced rules of speed are incredibly useful when the intention is to be in discovery-mode. But it's damaging in moments where you need to make significant decisions.

We too often prize decisiveness in leadership. We have inherited a belief that leadership is about fast and confident decision-making rather than deliberation and reflection. The phrase "any decision is better than no decision" feels intuitively right, even though—if you stop and think about it—any decision is clearly not better than no decision. When we make conversation, we're ultimately aiming not necessarily for action *but advancement.* Moving an idea forward, exploring that idea, but not necessarily just making it happen.

And when things go badly, we tend to speed up, which often escalates a crisis rather than mitigating it. In the peak of crisis, people just can't process information rationally.

A Supreme Court hearing is deceptively fast. They typically last about an hour, with each side getting thirty minutes to present its case. The justices pepper the lawyers with dozens and dozens of questions, even during that short time frame. It's over before you know it.

But that's not the end of the discussion—it's only the beginning. There are days, weeks, or months of deliberation that follow. Individual justices hold informal conversations with their clerks. The justices have a formal conference where votes are taken and, finally, arrive at a decision. And then the final court opinion is crafted by a single justice, released before the end of term. So, while the oral argument may seem fast, the deliberation is quite slow and thoughtful.

If you think back to the last time someone asked for a minute of silence, you may remember just how long a minute can feel. When the former Surgeon General Vivek Murthy and his team were studying the epidemic level of stress and anxiety in

America, he started to reflect on ways to reduce stress in staff meetings that were all about stress. His solution was simple: a minute of silence. "You know, sometimes you'll do a five-minute meditation and it starts to feel like an eternity, the mind wanders, it's actually counterproductive, but a minute, a minute can be the perfect amount of time."

Silence can do more than reduce anxiety and stress in a conversation; it can impact creativity and openness and help avoid crisis thinking. The psychologist Olga Lehmann says that when faced with big life decisions, we feel the pressure to discuss and act. But her research shows silence activates our brain's "default mode network," which is the same part of the brain activated when we daydream or fantasize. Silence allows a moment for the brain to shift from immediate expression to creative reflection.

You can design such moments into your conversation. Often people will choose to start with a moment of silence, but try planning it later in a conversation. Put it about two-thirds of the way through the discussion, maybe forty minutes into an hour-long conversation. Reserve it, put it on an agenda. You're setting a peaceful interruption "time bomb." If you're willing to plan it now, it might reset the conversation for you later.

Speaking of, let's end the bad routine of all-day meetings.

In his book *When*, Daniel Pink talks about how our daily mood cycle lifts in the morning, steadily declines through the afternoon, only to peak again in the early evening. We know this, we feel this ourselves, and yet we routinely ignore the idea that our bodies may be complicit in making good or bad decisions. When we're stuck in all-day meetings, we usually end up having our most important conversations in the 2:00 to 6:00 p.m. window—the moments when we're least able to apply energy and focus to the conversations that need them.

So, when asked to design conversations, I come back to the client with a simple constraint: multiple shorter conversations over multiple days and all of them end by 2:00 p.m. In order to get decisive action out of a conversation, the most effective move might be the most counterintuitive. These smart stops give your most important conversations the break they deserve.

I find that the first session can put a lot on the table; it can sprawl. Typically, the first day can lead to a bit of despair— sometimes even a lot of despair. That's why two hours is enough. The next day, when looking at the same set of possibilities and the same set of problems, it seems solvable, the path seems clearer after you've let the circumstances sit with the collective overnight.

Whether it's one minute or one night, constraints about slowness and smart stops aren't asking for a group to be any less decisive. They're just adding a small opportunity to reflect, and that will, in fact, ensure that the decision is better, sounder, and well thought through.

Constraints that Balance

One of the more interesting duels never fought was between then Illinois senator Abraham Lincoln and the politician James Shields.

The Code Duello—the set of rules governing the art of duels— had been established centuries earlier, but over successive years, the rules have shifted and evolved. Because in most cases the goal of the duel was to satisfy honor, not kill or even injure anyone. That's why there were rules like "first blood," which allowed challengers to declare victory if they even nicked an opponent.

By 1842, when Shields and Lincoln were to duel, it was common that the person challenged—in this case Lincoln— was the one to make up the rules of the duel. Lincoln, being Lincoln, established a fairly extreme and clever set of rules: he choose clunky and heavy military broadswords, and neither man could come within twelve feet of the other. In essence, he established a set of rules that ensured both men would make it through the duel unharmed. In the end, Shields and Lincoln were persuaded not to duel at all. Lincoln offered an apology and his challenger, Shields, accepted it in good humor.

I love this story, because it's a reminder that constraints can ensure that a conversation feels safe and fair. In essence, when Lincoln established his new dueling code, he was making it harder for the two in combat to hurt each other, actually for the most part removing the combative part of the duel.

It's important to remember that even if you feel free and safe in a conversation, there is a strong possibility someone else at the table feels less so—you may be surprised by who they are.

People often say things to me like "I want conflict in a conversation" or "I'm always open to good healthy debate." And it's often the case that people who want these things in a conversation feel highly equipped for debate or deft enough to navigate conflict. But that is very much not the case for all of us. A creative conversation can accommodate and respond to conflict, and it can make sure debate is "healthy." But to do so, there needs to be constraints in a conversation that provide the right kind of balance.

Can Critique Feel Good?

The idea of critique and how it happens well is an interesting analogue that allows us to explore how we can provide balance in a creative conversation.

In my work, and in much creative work, we continuously navigate around the need to give critique on a weekly, sometimes daily, basis. I've found that it's only through clear, articulated, and humane rules that critique can become an accepted part of the daily flow of work. Critical assessment is a necessary component of our day-to-day lives. It happens between teachers and students, employers and employees, within families. Sometimes critique entails one person giving feedback to another or to many, but a well-considered approach to the rules of how that happens can shift the feel of critique and increase everyone's comfort with it.

Given that we've just discussed time and pacing in a previous section, I won't belabor the fact that the most essential rules of critique center around when and how fast critique happens. Never offer critique the day before something is supposed to be done—that time frame is useless. No critique at the end of the day or the end of the week—those are the rules set by circadian rhythms. Choose instead the times our bodies and minds are most resilient. Schedule critique at the beginning of the day, not at the last exhausted moment left at the end of a long afternoon. And critique warrants real time spent on it. I often schedule ninety minutes for review and critique of ideas; it shifts the conversation from review to collective work.

But the most important element of critique is boundaries. So I start with questions that set the boundaries of what's up for review: *What do you love? What can't be touched? And what are the specific things you need help with?* This specifically establishes the terrain of the conversation, what can be worked on, and what needs to be left alone.

When you start a critique this way, you're giving the people about to be critiqued permission to set the constraints of what can be critiqued. It's a moment of collective negotiation that lays the ground for a safe, albeit challenging, conversation. This is really not that different from the Code Duello—the one challenged to the duel gets to set the rules for the duel.

Like anything, there are fads in the realm of critique and a tremendous amount of effort is put into leadership training on "how to give feedback." There are homespun methodologies, like "give a feedback sandwich"—a piece of critique between two points of praise. And there are the far more complicated frameworks like the two-by-two explored in *Radical Candor*. In my experience, little training on feedback can be a dangerous thing. Too often, leaders are taught to open with, "Can I give you some feedback?" But I've found that it's far better to ask, "Can I give you feedback on _____?" Make it specific. Like a design critique, it's helpful if you can point at "something" as opposed to "somebody."

One thing that happens when you open a critique with a question and invite someone to set the constraints is that it's perfectly reasonable for the other person to reply, "Not now." Constraints are not just about what you engage on, and how, but the "when" of engagement too. The benefit of establishing and co-creating constraints around critique is that it creates a balanced relationship and greater honesty can be achieved.

With the right constraints, a critique can shift from the realm of the painful to the relatively joyful. My editor and I have worked pretty closely for the last two years on this book about conversation, passing chapters back and forth. So, we have a fairly well-tuned set of constraints for our critique. Now he can write me a note about a chapter that says, "There's something wrong in your head." And not only do I agree, but I think it's funny. Constraints can absolutely set you free.

Constraints in Language

When I was in college, I took a course called Comparative Revolutions. Today I can't easily recall the theories of revolution, but I learned a very simple rule that has stuck with me. The professor, Darius Rejali, established that no student's comment could begin with the word *but*. It was Rejali's perspective that the word *but* signaled opposition and created a "conflict mentality" in the conversation.

By constraining the kinds of words we should be wary of, Rejali was in essence introducing a "tell" for conflict. With "buts" banned from the conversation, we were forced to reframe our comments, thus shifting the tenor of the conversation from opposition to collaboration.

Interestingly, the word *but* is also one of the words that is considered taboo in improvisational theater. Improv comedy relies on the constant interplay and collaboration of the performers and requires any idea introduced by one participant to be supported and built on by others—in essence, make the other performer look good. The word *but* is considered a language cue signaling that another performer might be breaking down someone's idea rather than building it up.

Calling out words and phrases that might signal negative connotations allows you to separate language from the person who is using it.

Establishing tells doesn't just have to be keeping an eye out for specific words; it can apply to subtler behavior as well.

I worked with a complex nonprofit organization, and one day, when one of the leaders was in the middle of a rambling monologue, he abruptly stopped himself and said, "Waste." At least that's what I thought he said. It turns out, he meant WAIST. It was an acronym.

I asked what it stood for. WAIST is a form of question: "Why am I still talking?" It was a constraint the organization had developed, so that you would interrupt yourself when you were off on a wander, when what you were saying was not necessarily moving a conversation forward, when you weren't adding anything.

And this is the one time I'm going to break my own rule about acronyms, because WAIST works. You hear what it means once and it sticks, and it almost immediately shifted the way I thought about my participation.

Not all conversations you will have in your life will be balanced. But the conversations that matter most to you should. Constraints are there precisely to help you do that.

Rethinking Constraints

In 1966 Yoko Ono exhibited an artwork called *White Chess Set*. True to its name, it consisted of a chess set where the board and the pieces were all white. Beneath the set was an inscription: "Chess set for playing as long as you can remember where all your pieces are." It was a profoundly simple antiwar piece, because those new constraints transformed chess from a game of battle to one where the battle could never be won. You could only play, for as long as you remembered.

In 2015, for an exhibition of Ono's work, the Museum of Modern Art reproduced the piece so that visitors could actually try it out. Wendy Woon, the curator of education, discovered that as people began to lose track of their pieces, they didn't stop playing—they began to discuss new rules for play. They established new and often collaborative goals that allowed the game to continue. What's more, they began having open and dynamic conversations about the political intention of the original piece. They changed the constraints.

It's an almost perfect illustration of my final point: Don't just set constraints and assume they're working. Take a Constraint Break. Take pauses in the conversation and build moments into a conversation to assess whether the rules are working. If not, consider what could change to make them work better. Just like building a moment of silence into an agenda, planning for a moment to consider the constraints, to understand how to make them work to best effect, can be useful.

When Andrea Lein of the John Dewey Academy took over, she described a kind of rule overload. Throughout the decades, rules had accumulated on top of more rules on top of more rules. Some were cardinal, like "No drugs." But others were unclear: "Only one person allowed in the laundry room at a time." So she did a rule purge, eliminating them all and starting over with a fresh slate.

After all, rules are not things. You don't make them and then sit with them forever. Rules are the software of the conversation: they can be written, tried, and then rewritten. One of the biggest risks to a creative conversation is treating rules as fixed as opposed to a set of constraints to be experimented with, used, and then removed when and if they don't work for the desired effect.

Making Conversation: The Hunch Hour

I first encountered what I call "Hunch Hour" in a workshop conducted by writer and political activist Courtney E. Martin on how to write an opinion piece. It was so good, I almost immediately stole the idea and used it myself. The game was the opening session of a multiday gathering and, in essence, it was a way to test op-ed ideas for their newsworthiness and relevance.

The session started by asking a group to go around the table and throw out a hunch. It could be something personal or focused on a specific topic. The hunch could be as simple as

"People stay up late in New York," to more complex ideas like "We no longer care about truth."

Then she would ask others around the table to "confirm" or "complicate" it. In order to do so, you had to offer evidence for or against the hunch. The evidence could be a scholarly article on the topic or something you had experienced firsthand. You could not confirm or complicate unless you had evidence.

That's the way the Hunch Hour worked. In the hour of conversation, people would share their ideas with the room and, depending on the feedback, they would pursue the idea further in writing or drop it entirely. This is not brainstorming—it's almost the opposite. Rather than throwing out wild ideas, this session is about taking half-formed ideas and giving them more weight and more evidence to work with. It is about propelling interesting ideas forward.

While I "borrowed" this conversation format and have used it successfully for years, I wanted to get a sense of where the inspiration for it came from, so I contacted Courtney for those details.

Hunch Hour is a perfect example of making conversation; in fact it's by nature a conversation that builds from our explorations of clarity, commitment, and constraints. Courtney had a set of goals she wanted to achieve. She wanted to give participants feedback on possible essay ideas. But she also wanted to get a group new to each other to connect. She wanted a playful tone, and language is essential here: the word *hunch* is not too weighty. If you shifted the word to *hypothesis*, nobody would want to participate. You don't lightly share a hypothesis with a room full of strangers, and you likely don't judge someone's hypothesis lightly.

Likewise, the words *confirm* and *complicate* are well chosen. This is not agreeing or disagreeing. *Confirm* and *complicate* are gentle. They point in a direction but they're not absolute. "A lot of the participants were academics, you know," Courtney told me, "so their tendency is to critique an argument, and I really wanted to avoid that behavior." Which, by the way, is why I've seen this work so well with foundations and philanthropies; the same tendency toward critique is embedded in the culture.

The time constraint of an hour is perfect too: enough time to cover a bunch of ideas without getting mired down. And the requirement of supportive evidence allows the conversation to advance an idea. You can complicate and confirm but only with a meaningful contribution of content that is essential. The rule here encourages participation but makes the participant complicit in the quality and development of the ideas of others.

In essence, much of this entire book is about constraints. Constraints can allow for more balance and freedom, but they can do much more; they can help you move toward specific goals and establish a specific tone. And, most important, as we saw with that grade school classroom, constraints might just help you get to that dream you've articulated.

Conversation Break: Taking Games Seriously

The issues we're exploring—new rules, new positions, new spaces, movement, and new modes of listening—are the foundation of what makes a good game work. For that reason, I often go to games for inspiration when I'm designing formats for productive conversations.

What follows are five things I've learned by taking games seriously.

1. GAMES PERSIST

Games are indicators of what is appropriate to discuss in a society at any moment, but the structure of some games we have today has existed for thousands of years. They reflect a long history of the ways humans haven chosen to interact.

When I spoke with Jim Stern, game designer and now head of game acquisition at Zynga, the electronic game distributor, he gave a broad and simple framework for how games evolve. According to him, there are really three typologies of games: the proven games that we know and that always persist; the better games that improve or alter the proven, but still work from the same game principles; and brand-new inventions, which are, in fact, rarer than you think.

The "proven" and the "better" categories of games, in particular, give clues that can be used when you think about how you might design dialogue. A simple example would be capturing the flag, which has been played by countless children for at least two centuries. Some believe that the game was directly adapted from actual military battles where capturing the enemy's flag was a signal that the battle was over.

In my childhood, Capture the Flag was a huge, sprawling game played over as many as eight city blocks and could go on well into the night. While this kind of play probably doesn't exist today, the game has evolved and been replaced by new and "better" versions. For example, I've seen it adapted by a husband-and-wife team who use it for corporate team building. They stage Capture the Flag games for adults in places like Grand Central Terminal. Changing the place, who plays, and the goals actually makes the game a means of teaching collaboration and communication skills.

2. GAMES TEACH

A game can teach economic theory, as Elizabeth Magie's *The Landlord's Game* was designed to do. It can teach morals, like the eighteenth-century *The Mansion of Happiness: An Instructive Moral and Entertaining Amusement.* Sometimes a game just teaches facts that will stick with you forever—useful or not—as anyone who has played *Trivial Pursuit* can attest to.

Monopoly, which was invented in 1935 and was an improved version of *The Landlord's Game*, is now played all over the world and in many different guises—you can find a *Star Wars Monopoly* right next to a *Junior Monopoly* or *Monopoly Frozen Edition* at any Target. The game remains fresh and pertinent not because of nostalgia or lessons about marketplaces but because it teaches us more fundamental skills: the art of negotiation, deal making, and strategic partnering.

Find a group and play the game again and you will discover— or remember—that the skill to *Monopoly* is knowing when to trade, when to give, when to negotiate and collaborate with other players to achieve the ultimate goal of owning the board. What if you applied these same skills to making conversation? Where would those skills feel appropriate, where would they be distracting?

3. GAMES SHIFT POWER

Games are simple ways of practicing new rules and shifting power roles. The Game of Courtly Love—popular among the aristocracy in the Middle Ages—was a game where women would challenge the male courtiers to convince them of their love by requiring these men to entertain them with some form of oratory. This game established a skill set that was important at the moment: how to be compelling and persuasive with words that mattered in a court setting. Even more important, however, the game reversed traditional power structures, allowing a moment where control was in the hands of the women of the court. They became arbiters of what was clever and smart in that context.

We don't have to look far to find games that similarly shift the balance of power today. One of the most "proven" parlor games is charades, in which an individual has to act out a saying or title using no words while a group tries to guess what they're trying to portray. Games like *Pictionary* are a "better" version of the game; the individual is given some title or concept and is required to express it to a group in the form of a drawn picture. The premise that makes these games work is that they take a common skill away from a collective of people, in this case words.

Charades works because it levels the playing field—commonly referred to as "handicapping." This leveling means that people who may be particularly good at one thing—words, in this case—cannot rely on those strengths, while others who may be better at physical expressiveness, or in the case of *Pictionary*, visual language, temporarily have an advantage.

In the same way, you might apply handicapping to making conversation when the participants aren't equal or when they aren't all starting on the same footing. Imagine what might happen if you stopped a conversation and asked someone to explain their point with no words. What might happen if you asked people in a room to move closer to or farther from someone the more they agree or disagree with them.

4. GOOD GAMES HAVE GOOD PRINCIPLES

At their root, games are play. They can be competitive and challenging, but they are also meant to be fun. A game does not have to be stupid or silly to still feel like play.

"New Games" were invented in the 1970s to be played in huge groups working toward a common goal—things like collectively moving a giant ball representing the earth across a field without it touching the ground.

Stewart Brand, the man behind *The Whole Earth Catalog*, also created one of the first "New Games." In a treatise he wrote, he called out what he saw as the five principles of a good New Game, which can be applied to making good conversation too—not to mention making a good life. They are: Forgiveness, Suspense, Keen Competition, Wit, and Ritual.

5. SOMETIMES GAMES ARE THE CONVERSATION

Jim, the game designer from Zynga, told me that when he was an awkward preteen, he used to come home from school and the first thing his mother would do was ask him to sit down with her and play a round of cards. It wasn't until years later that he realized that during the simple but distracting time spent in card play, he and his mother would have fairly intimate conversations about what was going on in his school and social life. That subtle distraction of game play—something akin to conditions of mesmeric listening discussed in chapter 2, "Creative Listening"—allowed him to open up in ways he might otherwise not have. It's a practice he continues with his own kids on the awkward first day back from college.

One of the best things we can learn about conversation from games is that you can win or lose a game, but it's still just a game. For the most part—there are exceptions—we don't hold grudges long about the games we lose. It's for that reason I urge us to look at what makes a game work that might in fact apply to conversation. When you start to take games seriously, it's surprising that we don't look to them more often to inspire the conversations we have.

CHAPTER 6
CHANGE

There are moments that remind us that
we all come from the same source.

—*Rhiannon Giddens*

We were all pretty shocked and embarrassed. We just sat
through the first twenty minutes in silence, but we persisted."

Donaree, a seventy-four-year-old self-described devout Christian in Salt Lake City, was telling me about when her book group
watched *Deep Throat*, the infamous porn film from the 1970s.

It began "innocently" enough. Donaree was playing bridge
with her husband and a collection of friends when someone
mentioned an article they'd read about hardware stores across
the country running out of rope—all because of this new book
Fifty Shades of Grey. One of the women mentioned that she'd
been on a waiting list for it at the library; yet another had gotten the whole series for Christmas. That afternoon, they decided

they would pull together a small collection of women and read the book together.

A few of the women knew each other well; others were friends of friends; all of them were between their fifties and seventies. They came from fairly conservative religious upbringings. Many were faithful Christians, Methodists, and Catholics; one even ran a local Christian charity.

"That first conversation was so much fun. It was a magic thing, actually, the gateway to have a conversation on this topic," said Donaree. "When we started talking, we realized there was a lot of stuff in that book we just have never even heard of, right? So, we just started asking each other questions. 'What do you think that's about? What about this?' Then a couple of months go by and we read the second one and get together."

The conversations progressed; they started in a place of just trying to understand, literally understand, what was happening in the books and gradually began to help them understand their own feelings about what happened.

Then they watched *Deep Throat*. Afterward, they became curious about the woman who starred in that film and went on to watch *Lovelace*, a biopic on the star of *Deep Throat*, Linda Lovelace, which centers around the profound negative impact that movie had on her life.

Those two films marked a moment when the conversation began to turn from the excitement of discovering sexuality to beginning to understand the exploitation of sexuality, the persecution of nonconforming gender identities, and increasingly moved toward more complex and nuanced conversations.

"After that, we kind of discarded the books," said Donaree.

"We became a group of six women that started talking about things that are probably on a lot of women's minds but never, ever comes out of their mouths because there's never an opportunity to say things or ask questions."

Change is an essential component of making conversation—in many cases, it is the goal of a creative conversation. Serious, hard conversations that don't enable some form of change are, unfortunately, just serious and hard conversations.

That's why I love the story of Donaree's book club.

First, their experience helps us define what we mean by change. I've spent a long time grappling with that definition, and recently I thought back to an interview I'd done with the playwright Lisa Kron months earlier on the idea of catharsis. You may remember this concept from high school English class: it's a moment in theater that inspires a release of "pity and fear." When I mentioned it as a critical component of change, she just brushed the idea aside; I think it seemed a bit heady to her. She offered a much more beautiful and simpler approach.

"Catharsis," she said, "is really just a moment of collectively showing up."

Her words came back to me and created a moment of clarity. The kind of change I was looking for was change that forged a collective. I was looking for a moment that said we showed up for one another and now we're moving forward together. It is ultimately that building of a collective that allows us to imagine and create the future we want to inhabit.

Second, Donaree and her friends *noticed* they were changing. Each time they recognized that they felt different, more knowledgeable, and engaged on the topic. It's important to recognize that it was the books and films at the center of their club that helped them progress—in essence, motivating that change. "After reading *Fifty Shades of Grey*, we just had so many questions"—that's a reaction to the book, a need to understand a kind of curiosity. But if they hadn't also been so remarkably aware that the book had provoked a change, *and they liked it*, they would not have been in a place to continue making conversation in the first place.

As Donaree said to me toward the end of our conversation, "Moments that are full of potential for connection happen all the time, to everybody, in little specific groups. You find yourself in spaces with specific groups a lot of times, but if you're not aware, they just pass by. How full your life would be if you'd grab onto those moments when they happen."

Noticing that change has happened, and finding some way to surface that change, the nature of it, and perhaps marking it so you can continue to elevate the conversation, is something that can be done purposefully. There are tools at our fingertips that are built for exactly that; they can help us see change and use that change to go further, and many of them are found in age-old human ritual. What we want to start to explore as we look at change are the tools that help prepare us for change, notice change, and then finally move on to the next big change in our conversation.

Explore, Reflect, Advance . . . Change

At our farm upstate, I walk the perimeter of the property—about a mile—every day. It's remarkably routine, a bit dull, deeply meditative. But after doing it for five years now, what I really notice is *change*.

One day, a field has more yellow flowers than red; one day, the forest floor is covered with ivy; one day, the wind makes the forest shake and crack; one day, it's silent and breezeless; all I see is change. So too with well-made conversations that happen again and again: they reveal change.

I believe that's why Donaree's book group worked. Not because the format or design of the conversation was so spectacular, but in fact because it was so mundane. There is no work, no surprise in the format of a book group. Pick a book, read a book, discuss a book, and see what happens. In Donaree's context, though, it seems outrageous; it was actually *even more routine*—after all, the first rule of sex book club is that the book has to be about sex. But that's the magic, no reinvention, always the same theme, always the same format, so what they noticed when they reflected was one thing and one thing only: the change in them.

Explore, reflect, advance, and change.

Given that this is a book about getting creative with conversation, it may be surprising that I advocate for sometimes very familiar and routine structures when you want to see change. But like anything, seeing change requires practice, and the more familiar some of the structures are, the easier it can be to spot change when it happens.

Some of the formats I write about in the book—like Hunch Hour or Whine and Dine—are designed conversations that I've been in many hundreds of times, and that's on purpose. It's not just that once something works, it's worth holding on to.

Because those formats are now so familiar to me, I can participate and see change when it happens. I've used them enough that I know what it looks like and I know where in the conversation to call out that change has happened.

In fact, over the years I've altered formats in order for them to feel more familiar to people. When I go into strategy planning with clients and teams, I always do short micro-interviews, about thirty minutes long, with everyone involved. Years ago, when I started this practice, it was common for me to ask, "How did you get to where you are?" but in the last few years, and because of the rise of the Marvel Universe (yes, really), I've started these conversations by asking for their origin story.

I do that because it's a format almost everyone knows and it's also a format that asks for them to call out change. Think about it: normal human, bitten by a radioactive spider, changed to hero; normal Amazon, falls in love and leaves the island, becomes hero. Change is implicit and you always get the storyteller to identify the moment of change in their lives.

So I don't just want you to design conversations, I want you to practice conversation. Choose a few formats, constraints, or tools you like and work with them over and over again. It's not about getting good at the format—or rather, it's not just about getting good at the format; it's about letting the conversation feel so familiar and routine that it can fall to the background and you can start getting good at change-spotting.

That said, let's also look at some practices that specifically help us make or mark change.

Motivating Change: Go on a Pilgrimage Together

We sat in the stone plaza of the Cathedral of Santiago de Compostela. More accurately, we were sprawled out on the stone plaza. Our shoes were off; our pants were rolled up to our knees; our bruised toes wiggled in the chill fall air. We sat quietly, dazed, and then spontaneously falling into silent convulsing tears.

Early in my research, I sought out moments where people reported deep connections to others and bonds that lasted—specifically, the kinds of conditions that lead to commitment among groups of people. That was how my husband and I found ourselves on a ten-day 140-mile pilgrimage on the Camino de Santiago to the cathedral.

We were exhausted, almost broken by the as much as twenty miles a day of walking. We'd been exposed to the remarkable beauty—fairy-tale paths through woodland and forest—and perils—torrential freezing rain and mud—of the landscape of northeast Spain. We were heartened by the warmth and openness of the people we met along the way, many of whom we knew now by face if not by name. Finally, after walking through the final miles of dull urban sprawl, the back end of the airport, even we were confronted with the spectacular awe of the cathedral. We found ourselves among the crowd laughing, crying, embracing, and full of abundant joy. We had, in the end, become pilgrims, not observed them.

The three miles we had just walked had been through gray suburban sprawl; my husband was in extreme pain from shin splints and the reemergence of an old knee injury. We really just wanted it over. We eventually found our way into the cobbled streets of the city center where the scallop shell signs that had guided us for the last five days and one hundred miles—approximately a fifth of the full Camino—were obliterated by tourists and locals setting up shop.

Pushing on, we walked down a grand set of stairs under a giant arch and found ourselves in the huge expanse of the plaza. The space was what you might imagine to be a renaissance painter's vision of the architecture of heaven. The crowd seemed to be mingling like at one giant party, as they wandered barefoot through the plaza; they laughed and cried and spontaneously hugged fellow pilgrims and complete strangers.

We had *changed*.

The basic tenets that underlie all pilgrimage, sacred or not, are simple. The singular point to pilgrimage is that you are going to a holy place, a place that has some form of sanctity and spiritual meaning. This means the path of the pilgrim is directional; there is only forward.

Pilgrims are expected to endure some form of hardship and some form of a journey. Pilgrimage removes one from daily life and daily experience. Finally, a pilgrimage ends with a unifying of the many into one. The most common metaphor is the language of water: brooks join to streams, which join to rivers, and finally, as Martin Luther King Jr. put it, into a "giant wave of people."

More important, pilgrims all walk with *an expectation of change*. While pilgrimage is a thing and action, you find that the term is often used for any form of journey—metaphorical or real—where some form of transformation is expected. Not only is there personal change but the bonds between pilgrims who walk with each other—even for short periods—are remarkably strong. As one handbook for pilgrims states: "The destination—the shrine, a holy mountain, or a house of goal—will signify not the end of a journey, but the start: a gateway into a new way of being, of seeing life afresh with spiritually cleansed eyes."

Early in the civil rights movement Martin Luther King Jr. often used the term *pilgrimage* instead of *protest*; his first thirty-thousand-person gathering in Washington, DC, in 1957, was officially called "The Pilgrimage to Freedom." And it's important to note that almost all of the protests of this era, like the marches on Washington or to Selma, had destinations. People were going somewhere and with that came an implicit or explicit promise of change.

That's part of the reason that the protests happening in the wake of George Floyd's murder feel so different from, say, the meaningful but diffuse-feeling Women's March. These Black Lives Matter rallies, which seem to have transformed everything overnight, have a specific destination, a goal, a demand: defund the police. Even distributed and under lockdown, these protesters are going somewhere.

Likewise, in my research I often found that anytime people discussed lengthy and hard processes, where there is effort, real time is spent, and change happens, it was likely the term *pilgrimage* would arise. Casper ter Kuile, one of the hosts of the podcast *Harry Potter and the Sacred Text*, studies replacements for religion in increasingly secular cultures: what allows us to build community in contexts where there is no religion; what allows us to forge on common values when religion can't. Not surprisingly, Casper is someone I go to when I want to understand all things sacred.

At breakfast recently, Casper was telling me about the time he and a group of friends watched all eight of the Harry Potter films over eight weeks, using them as a structure for deep conversation. As he talked about the session, I was struck when he used the term *pilgrimage*. I asked him why that word, and he paused.

"Um, I guess pilgrimage is always a place where that's where the established social hierarchies have to be disbanded because everyone is walking on foot, everyone needs to eat and sleep," he explained. "It's this very equalizing experience, especially if traveling, but what's important is that it allows us to step outside of our normal everyday life and enter the river of time in a different way. So, on the Wednesday morning when we had watched the first three movies, three Wednesdays in a row, and I knew the next one was coming, I felt like I was within a bigger journey, part of the longer arc. It wasn't just a random Wednesday."

This is what I learned from my study of pilgrimage: Setting a destination is an optimistic act. Establishing a goal, and working with a group to get there, gives that group a greater potential for achievement—for change. Our daily lives are established by a pattern of meetings and tasks, and it's not uncommon to lose the goal. Daily life is the opposite of directional.

Creative conversations, like pilgrimages, are going to be arduous, they are going to test us, sometimes they might bore us or break us. But if they have a stated goal and an intention, if there's a feeling that there is only forward, only the future, then you as a group will experience true change. It doesn't require you to walk one hundred miles together or do a two-month movie marathon. It simply requires you to set a destination together, do whatever it takes to get there, and don't stop until you do. Trust me, along the way, you'll show up for another.

Motivating Change: How Did *Fifty Shades of Grey* Make Conversation?

There has been a notable rise in book clubs at the same time that we're supposedly experiencing a decline in dialogue. It's an interesting sign for us, because obviously a book club uses the book as an impetus for gathering, and it can be an excuse to have conversations you might not have typically. Donaree and her friends didn't decide to get together and talk about sex—in fact, they would have likely rejected that idea outright. Rather these women got together to talk about this new book *Fifty Shades of Grey*, and that book led them through a change; it actually helped motivate that change.

In a book club, in a visit to a museum, seeing a controversial film, you are given a way to objectify an issue, a set of beliefs, or choices. Exploring our collective reaction to a text or any form of art is a way to build bonds and community, but it's also a way to begin to explore deep beliefs, and even change them. We have *always* used art, theater, film, literature, and—yes—holy writings to explore difficult subjects and host change across cultures and across history; it's just something humans seem to do. Discussing a book or a prayer or a film allows for the same behaviors we exhibit when we participate in a well-run critique:

it gives us something to discuss and even judge without judging each other.

Take the Passover Seder, for instance. The Haggadah, the text that is read over the course of the meal, sets the Passover agenda. It tells the story of the Jews' freedom from slavery and their subsequent flight across the desert. The Seder is highly structured with questions about the ritual itself that remind those gathered of their history; specific foods are served that represent the trials and triumphs of their flight; even the notion of eating in a reclined position is a reminder of what it means to be free—slaves ate standing.

It's a guide to what will be discussed and when it will be discussed; it establishes a set of constraints on time and pacing. The Haggadah describes a common history shared by Jewish people, but the rituals associated with this commemoration inevitably tie us to current events in a visceral, concrete way. Remembering the expulsion of the Jews from Egypt is not quite the same as just discussing immigration policy at the dinner table, but it's close, and often you'll find that the historical frame gives you a way to explore an immediate issue.

When working with clients, I often recommend using some form of text as the backdrop for a hard conversation. But, quite honestly, clients tend to resist this approach: "It's too much like a classroom," or "We don't want to give people homework." But, as I try to point out to clients, a good conversation is in many ways like a classroom: classrooms allow a diverse set of people to have hard and exploratory conversations, and they often use texts as a structure to explore those ideas. Yes, using a text *is* reminiscent of a classroom and that's *exactly the point.*

Let's look at Casper's podcast, which he created with Vanessa Zoltan. In 2017 *Pottermore*, the official website of all things Harry Potter, reported that 500 million copies of the books had sold in more than eighty different languages, which means that approximately one in fifteen households in the world have a Harry Potter book. The book has been read by enough people to establish a common language—a common set of reference points and areas of exploration that can cut across cultural and religious barriers.

Each episode of *Harry Potter and the Sacred Text* takes one chapter from the Harry Potter books and extracts the broader moral or emotional implications; the podcast hosts explore themes in the chapter, as well as readings sent in from listeners around the world. With their podcast, Vanessa and Casper are showing just how texts can help us explore change.

As Casper said, "You're going from a narrative reading to a sort of imaginative phase, to making it personal, to making it actionable. The point of a sacred reading like this is you're supposed to be changed by it; it's supposed to be a transformative process. It might be a very small action: 'I'm reminded that I love my sister, I'm going to give her a call.' But we've also had listeners write in and say, 'This made me decide that I was going to finally adopt a child.'"

Not long after I spoke with Casper, I was asked by the managing publisher and the managing editor of a local news organization to design a conversation for them that would help guide them through a moment of perceived cultural rift. The organization had only been publishing for five months, but there seemed to be a growing disagreement about what kinds of stories they should be covering. This was a conversation that required both strategic decisions and the building of a collective around those decisions. It was a conversation that required change.

There was no way in the world I wanted to facilitate a free-form conversation with an unhappy newsroom; I've seen those and it's always a bit dicey. But I was happy to design a series of conversations for them using different kinds of constraints, for them to have together. Remember, the idea with making conversation is that we design them, not facilitate them. I thought I'd use the opportunity to experiment with the idea of using a text to create collective understanding and change as a way to advance the conversation.

One of the methods Casper told me about was Lectio Divina—literally, divine reading. It's a traditional monastic way of studying scripture. A reader chooses a paragraph from a text, originally the Bible, and reads it four different ways. In essence, you place four different constraints on the reading. In a traditional Lectio Divina, first you read for facts: "What's happening?" Second, you read and compare it to some other work of art, a fable, a myth, or story. Third, you relate it to your own life: "When have you experienced something similar?" Last, you ask yourself what God is telling you to do.

It's not just the content of the text but *the way the text is read* that encourages the potential for change.

Because the primary source of conflict in this group was the columns and stories they themselves were writing, the "sacred text" seemed obvious. I asked that every staff member choose one story that had been published that, for them, exemplified the ideal story. When they gathered, I had them read it, Lectio Divina–style with a few modifications.

First, I asked what the story was literally about. Second, what that story was like, and if there were other stories in the world it reminded them of. On the third and fourth reading, I diverged more significantly from Lectio Divina, establishing different constraints. I asked them to do a third reading that examined what the story made them feel. For the final question, I asked: "What did the story tell you about what else you should be publishing in the future?" I watched them nervously hunched over their iPhones, reading and rereading their chosen stories, preparing their critiques. But when they began to share, a moment of surprising change occurred.

Though there were thirty journalists in the room, they had chosen pretty much the same five stories.

Immediately they knew the kinds of stories that mattered to them: typically, something championing the underdog. Their perspective was more alike than they thought.

Furthermore, when they discussed the third reading—"How did the story make you feel?"—the universal emotion was "outrage." As they discussed the feeling, they collectively agreed that they didn't want to be a news outlet fueled by outrage.

When they discussed the fourth reading—"What did this story tell you about what to do in the future?"—much of the conversation was about doing more solution-based stories, stories that helped people navigate hard-to-manage systems. They wanted to celebrate the underdog and how they prevailed, with an emphasis on celebration, not injustice.

The reading motivated and made change for the group. They

realized that there was less division among the group than they had thought, but they also realized how they wanted to change their stories going forward. Not only did they "show up," as Lisa Kron described, but they did so and chose a new path forward. They advanced.

What's especially intriguing about a reading practice like Lectio Divina is that the text in the end may be somewhat arbitrary. The act of purposefully reading a passage, together, and reading it for all the various meanings it might hold, or all the interpretations the individuals in a room might have, encourages a moment of collective reflection. While the passage can be random, the intention is to create a collective conversation on that passage. This work of interpretation—of collective interpretation—shifts the focus of the room from individual meaning to the exploration of the meanings held by many.

You might have a sacred text in your home or your workplace and not even realize it. I work with many organizations that continue to refer back to their founding mission statements, as they project themselves forward and plan for the future. On the board of National Public Radio, we continually refer back to the founding charter forty years later; we try to check our aspirations against that original document. In many cases words of the founders are the closest we have to a "sacred text." I've heard Walmart employees refer back to Sam Walton's biography, *Made in America*, as a lens to help them make decisions today. In your family, it might very well be Harry Potter or the Passover Haggadah.

Marking Change: Making Conversation

So here's the dilemma: we only know that we've made conversation if we've felt a change in ourselves and the group. But change, no matter how big, is so easy to miss. Unlike Donaree and her book club, we often let it pass us by. What's more, there's no predictable or obvious moment when change happens. It's not always at the end of a conversation; sometimes it can happen in the first few minutes, or in some odd and unexpected instant.

One of the easiest ways to spot change is to think back to Lisa Kron's notion of "collectively showing up." And it's something you often feel rather than just see. It's common to feel it happen when experiencing music, theater, or religious moments where the group is kind of transported one level up—in music this moment of transcendence and unity often accompanies a modulation, literally a change of key; so too in conversations you can feel and see when there's been that change of key.

Amelia Winger-Bearskin noticed a change when she decided to sing that lullaby in a meeting; there had been a modulation down and she changed the key and brought us together by singing. She marked a change and then made a change. So too did Donaree; she noticed when conversations started to feel less scary and less definitional in her book group and she built on that. While change was happening all the time, the night they watched *Deep Throat* they definitely changed the key of that conversation group.

When you feel group lightness and hear group laughter,

that's a likely sign that change happened to seize on it. So too when you see group sadness and despair; another kind of change has happened there, so make sure to notice it. One of the reasons I love the conversation format we'll explore at the end of this chapter—creative tensions—is because it's all about learning to feel change and then using that change to force us to collectively show up.

I implore you then: keep an eye out for change, and then *talk* about it. Change needs to be acknowledged and celebrated— only then can you experience the kind of shift that propels us forward to action and, ultimately, to creation.

There are many ways you can "mark" change when it happens. And they can be very simple.

SIMPLE ACTS OF MARKING CHANGE

In the late 1960s, artist Mierle Laderman Ukeles wrote *Manifesto on Maintenance Art*, which called out that most forms of caretaking—maintenance, sanitation, for instance—are at best invisible in our culture, if not actually actively reviled. Her work documented the jobs of housecleaners and sanitation workers, jobs that were purposely unseen and unrecognized.

New York then was on the decline, epitomized by eroding infrastructure, near bankruptcy, and a series of sanitation strikes that had built tension between city workers and city residents. Moved to action, the artist wrote a letter to the New York Department of Sanitation suggesting they establish an artist-in-residence program with her to help de-escalate tensions through a series of collaborations between her, the city, and its sanitation workers. The department agreed, and Mierle still retains her artist-in-residency position with the sanitation department more than fifty years later.

Over the collaboration, the artists and the department have put on garbage fleet ballets, where talented drivers perform astonishing dance moves. Together, they "bejeweled" garbage trucks, transforming them into reflective mirrors that traveled the city, reminding citizens of their inescapable connection to their own trash and the critical role the city's workers played in making their lives better.

These projects—in essence, fifty years of creative conversations among the city, its citizens, and its sanitation workers—started with a simple handshake, albeit nine thousand hands.

It was simple. Mierle visited every part of the sanitation system and greeted every single sanitation worker with a handshake and a thank-you, in this case: "Thank you for keeping New York City alive." There was something so radical in her physical acknowledgment of sanitation workers as human beings. Photos show surprised, sometimes bemused, but often proud and happy (mostly) men shaking hands with the artist. It was a dramatic act, marking that a change was underway.

Consider how you might use such physical acts of connection to mark change. Similarly, church services often close with parishioners turning to greet those next to them, exchanging handshakes or even hugs. I'm not a religious person, but I always feel elevated in that last moment. Small moments don't just mark change—sometimes they make change.

Or remember back to the conversation break on peaceful interruption; much of it was focused on breaking a moment when things felt like they might be veering off. Peaceful interruption is really a perfect tool to help you mark change. We often pause conversations to ask, "How are we all feeling?" But instead consider asking, "What's happening here?"

Make this question a kind of refrain and it will allow you as a group to keep tabs on where a conversation is and where it's going. The right question at the right moment is likely to help you spot change.

TAKING A VOW

My friend Zia Khan, the senior vice president of the Rockefeller Foundation, recently introduced me to the concept of a "zombie coalition." Zombie coalitions, he says, are groups of people who get together to talk about a topic, agree to make change, don't, but then sort of shuffle forward assuming that those two actions have made them a movement. Does this sound familiar?

Taking a vow is one way to stop the Zombie Coalition Apocalypse.

A vow has a unique way of making change happen in a conversation, specifically when that vow is in support of or a way to honor specific actions or individuals. A public vow has the ability to clarify intention, galvanize support, and, at the right moment, create a community from what might otherwise be a collection of strangers.

Taking a vow has always been a means to mark change. This is why I love borrowing from ritual. Ritual often asks us to connect to our community in a specific way and typically, at the same moment, it's about awakening a connection to yourself, your meaning, and the things that matter most, and connecting that to a community of support or a community with the same goals.

But most important, integrating aspects of ritual into our conversations is a "proven" way for us to move a conversation forward. Proven because many of these practices have existed for thousands and thousands of years and continue to be practiced and continue to have effect.

Obviously, anyone who has participated in a wedding ceremony in any capacity has seen the power of "the vow" firsthand. Certainly, if you are the one being married, the significance of taking that vow is felt immediately. Even the most jaded people may find themselves moved by matrimonial vows. It's not for nothing that these vows are often taken in front of family and friends—a community who helps reinforce the change that has taken place. What's more, wedding vows are specific. Two people are committing to each other, and the community gathered are committing to help them maintain that commitment.

Celebration, vows, and encouragement are an essential component of change in part because they encourage us to see change when it happens. Celebrations and public encouragement are essential, but they don't mark *the end of a creative conversation*. There is still more work to do, and it may be the hardest work yet.

Vows can also be taken—or announced—by individuals. I once was in a meeting where the head of a cultural institution with considerable assets was asked to synthesize what he had heard from a couple days of shared research on the role of community and art. But instead of summarizing, he just made a vow, promising that his legal team would help set up a nonprofit to support continued research. That vow marked a change in the conversation and that vow actually catalyzed others in the room to follow up with further promises of support.

We miss something if we don't explicitly acknowledge when a room is in collective agreement. When that happens, try getting specific and asking for a commitment, a vow. It doesn't have to be dramatic moment. It can be as simple as a question posed to the group: "What are we willing to do to make this happen?"

Making Conversation: Creative Tensions

A couple years back, my IDEO team designed a conversation format that both hosted change and marked change. As with the *Fifty Shades* book club, that was absolutely not the original intention. Honestly, we just wanted to invent a dating game. A way for people to mingle and find others like themselves.

So about two months later, I found myself in a Lower East Side bar mingling with a crowd of about thirty "friends," who'd been invited to test a prototype for a new kind of conversation. There were no chairs, not one. Taped to the parquet floors was a huge green rectangle with a vibrant red dividing line down the middle. If anything, it was vaguely reminiscent of a basketball court. The collected participants were uncomfortable, but in an excited way. The panelists seemed equally uncomfortable.

On a long, narrow stage at one end of the room, there was a screen and in front of that screen was a comedian and an activist. At the back of the room was our "host." The comedian and activist were the panelists—actually we called them Catalysts, as their job was to catalyze a response from the audience; the host was playing the role of director and narrator.

The conversation started with a slide that said, "I am more Silk or Corduroy," with the two words on opposite sides of the screen. The audience and the provocateurs were asked to arrange themselves across the length of the room closest or farthest from the term that best defined them. The crowd did so and there was nervous laughter and chatter as people made their way across the room.

From here the tensions got harder. They were about power and who has it: "Power must be Given or Taken?" The room rearranged, and everyone from provocateurs to audience members were asked why they were where they were.

Next, "Power is about Words or Action." The room shifted yet again. As people positioned themselves, the host asked them why. Compelling stories were told, and people were encouraged to move closer if they related, farther if not. A deep conversation on a serious issue was had, but at the end of an hour when the conversation stopped, the buzz was loud and excited. I later heard that many people gathered in impromptu groups and went out to continue the conversation long into the night. Not just the conversation about power but the greater conversation about the role of tensions, good and bad, in conversation and in society.

I can't be sure, but I also suspect there might have been at least one or two hookups that night.

We called the conversation "Creative Tensions." It's a combination of a theater exercise, topics that are often considered polemic, and a practice called values clarification—which not surprisingly is most commonly used in kindergartens. And though it was originally built as a dating game, it's a powerful format that allows anyone to have very hard conversations about very hard topics in a way that is invigorating and connecting. I've done them on health, diversity and race, income inequality, and anxiety.

There's a lot in "Creative Tensions" that pulls broadly from all of the chapters: The context is changed, both the space and the position in space. There is just the right amount of constraints in place, and they are explained clearly and concisely.

And it's all designed to catalyze change: The tensions themselves are a new text that require interpretation. We're explicitly up front that we won't define the terms; everyone needs to do it for themselves. When you put a tension up, you can clearly see people stop and think about where they are on the spectrum. It's a beautiful thing, really, to see people reflect before they "choose sides."

Once they've positioned themselves, they are invited to explain why they're in the position they're in, why they believe that they're standing in the right place. As they speak to their position or tell the story of why they're there, you watch other people reflect again and sometimes move. The tensions invite people in and invite them to tell their own stories. So it really does encourage all the best parts of creative listening too.

And the movement marks when change happens. I've explored all kinds of theories about why the movement works, certainly there's an argument that some kind of "embodied cognition" is happening, but I'm not going to bother with something that sophisticated. Quite simply, movement marks a change of mind. As people talk and others move toward or away from each other—most often toward—there is a continual marking of change. You can see it happen. You move. Others move.

I've seen a woman explore the pain of losing her son to police violence and have people gather around her, including police officers, in the conversation. I've seen the joy of someone expressing a conservative viewpoint and people still show up for them. The exercise asks for people to share their emotions, to illuminate their lives, and when that happens, when those moments are felt, the conversation requires that people literally mark that change by gathering around them.

This is the perfect embodiment of Lisa Kron's notion of "collectively showing up for another." So often I hear that the conversation works for everyone precisely because you don't have to speak at all, ever, to feel like you've participated and been heard. Here, when people "show up," it's literal.

The dual components of "Creative Tensions"—motivating and marking change—elevate the conversation to a remarkable degree. It makes the conversation feel like something else entirely. Indeed, when we did one in Washington, just after the last election, almost two hundred people showed up from all kinds of political backgrounds to participate. It was dynamic, engaged, joyful even, despite the incredible political variations in the room. I ended the "Creative Tensions" with the same reminder that I always finish with: "Everything in life is in tension, everyone, every family organization or country is in constant tension.

The work of 'Creative Tensions' is to remind us that we can navigate them when we acknowledge they exist and are willing to discuss them as a collective."

When "Creative Tensions" end, the room is beyond buzzy; people are excited, they always say they wish for more than an hour—by the way, an hour is exactly right for that kind of conversation. The collective feeling of change and the rather abrupt ending makes people choose to continue the conversations on their own.

Afterward, someone grabbed me in tears and laughter and said, "That was my church." We set out to make a dating game, but we got something better.

Change is, in my mind, an elemental component of a creative conversation. Every aspect of this book suggests ways to make change happen, but unless there is a visible, out-loud moment that enables people to "collectively show up for each other," we miss the true joy that conversation can hold for us.

A moment of change designed into a conversation provides for a climax. But that climax is not about closure—it's about what's next. Marking change has the specific purpose of bonding a group of people in exploratory conversation into a community of action. It's only when this moment is observed that we can hope to move on to the most important potential outcome of a conversation: creation.

Conversation Break: Encouraging Encouragement

When I walked the pilgrim's way to Santiago de Compostela I noticed an interesting phenomenon. Every single pilgrim offers only encouragement, only words of support. When you think about it, that shouldn't be a surprise. Many of us were in pain, we were walking for as many as forty days in all kinds of weather, and we were all going to the same place—maybe for one time in our lives, everyone was traveling the same way. Encouragement, in that case, is the only option.

Think of conversation as a journey you're undertaking with others. You're all moving along in the same direction and a key component of making it to the end is stopping every once in a while, recognizing how far you've gotten, and encouraging each other to continue on.

It's important to call out that creative conversations require more than your average amount of encouragement. It's worthwhile being explicit on this point because we are celebrating out loud less and less. It's not just that hugs have been replaced by Instagram hearts. It's also the place where I recommend being the least creative. Keep positive in a conversation by being authentic and relying on age-old practices of encouragement, positivity, and a simple thank-you.

A while back, a team of designers took on a small conceptual project to look at the idea of why Mondays feel so joyless. We all know how it feels. The existential dread of Sunday night. The first shocking hours of Monday morning, readjusting to work. And the slow ease: "Oh right, there are people here I like." "Wait, there are parts of my job that are fulfilling."

The team invented a little practice: every Sunday night, they would send a message, just an email, to give encouragement for their week ahead. Perhaps it was someone who had done something helpful the week before; maybe just someone you hadn't been in contact with for a while. The subject line of this small praise-based email was always the same: "Open Monday Morning."

The act of sending a message was meant to encourage them on the beginning of their weekly journey. It turned out to have a significant emotional impact, helping not only those who received it but the person who sent it the night before.

It's simple, it works, try it.

The less creative you are with encouragement the better; it should feel robust and real. Applaud, cheer, slap each other five, hug, do things that normal people do when they're encouraging normal people on. Not surprisingly that kind of encouragement—simple, human to human, and genuinely expressed—triggers the body to release that "love hormone" oxytocin, which means that not only does encouragement keep you going, it connects you to people in the conversation more deeply.

CHAPTER 7

CREATE

> The future is not a result of choices among
> alternative paths offered by the present, but
> a place that is created—created first in mind
> and will, created next in activity. The future is
> not some place we are going to, but one we
> are creating. The paths are not to be found,
> but made, and the activity of making them
> changes both the maker and the destination.
>
> —*John Shear*

I'm ending the book where I begin most of the conversations I have in my life: I always start by reminding clients, teams, and collaborators that we can create our own future. Even if it seems hard, you're better off trying than not.

The point of making conversation is to be in conversation together, to make change together, and then make that change manifest. For some of us that means something very close in, like building a relationship dynamic. It could be bigger, but still within the realm of daily life—forging a work culture or heading down a different strategic path. Or it could be as big as moving a community forward. Right now, most of the conversations we have don't do that, even the conversations that matter most.

Above all, that was why, in seeking out inspiration for this book, I spent so much time talking to people from creative backgrounds: artists, filmmakers, designers, and writers. Simply put, creative people are compelled to create. It is the goal of their process. Lisa Kron, the playwright behind *Fun Home*, told me that when you're making a musical, or any collaborative work of art, there comes a moment when you just need to "make things out of what you have and where you are." That's it, exactly. You just need to make things out of what you have and where you are.

Let's be clear about one other point, which might seem ironic coming at the end of a book about conversation: there are times when talking just can't happen. All over America there are still stories about families that can no longer sit down to Thanksgiving and Christmas dinners together. Some communities are so divided, in the throes of painful rifts, that it's "too soon" to believe and hope for a healthy conversation. You may not be willing, and your neighbor may not be willing yet either.

That's perhaps the place where doing can have the most significant impact. You can clean up your countryside, quilt, sew, knit, build a barn, cook a giant meal, have a block party, serve Thanksgiving dinner. All of these things will build community and will build conversation even if you're not engaging with topics that divide the people who've gathered together.

So, when you can't talk, create.

Impatience Is a Virtue

In 2007 in Estonia, a small group of people had gathered to discuss growing concerns about pollution. For centuries, people had taken their trash to the forests and left it. But the nature of that trash had changed; it used to be waste that would disappear, perhaps even benefit the soil. But now, of course, trash was plastic, it was chemical, and suddenly forests were home to unused appliances, farm tools, and worse. When the group approached Estonian entrepreneur Rainer Nõlvak for support, he threw out a fairly audacious condition: the group would organize a cleanup of the entire country and they would do it in a single day.

Suddenly, a collection of people who had gathered to discuss a problem became a collective with a solution in mind.

The goal was, in many ways, impossible. Estonia is huge. And government policy requires that sanitation workers handle potentially hazardous trash; so compelling everyday citizens to clean up the country was not just difficult but in fact illegal. However, the group had committed, so they pushed hard and fast, setting a date for the cleanup essentially two months from the development of the idea. In the end, they got government approval by threatening that if there wasn't support for the cleanup, citizens would dump the trash on the steps of the nation's capital.

On May 3, 2008, fifty thousand Estonian citizens gathered across the country and just started picking up trash. Church groups, schools, competitive companies, entire families just started cleaning and, by the end of the day—no, really, in just five hours—the country was clean.

Rainer acknowledges that cleaning up was pretty exhausting: "We thought we were done with it. We were tired, we thought we were never going to touch trash again. And yet, this human resilience and craving for cleanliness just kept coming back." The group organized under the name Let's Do It—after all, they really had just done it—and they continued to clean Estonia yearly. You know things still get untidy. Today the country of Estonia, approximately 1.3 million people, has inspired more than 18 million people around the world to take on their own large-scale, short-time-frame cleanup.

I've been telling this story for years because it's so spectacular, until you realize that maybe it isn't—maybe it's just human nature. There is a profound sense of accomplishment and collectivity that happens when you achieve something seemingly impossible and you do it fast.

When you set impossible deadlines to make something real happen in the world, so many of the barriers to good conversations disappear. Many of the questions that hang us up—"What are we talking about?" "Are we in agreement?" "Do we think this is the right direction?"—shift into only one question: "How are we going to do this?" When "how" becomes the root of the conversation and the time becomes constrained, the tone shifts. How and how fast generate help.

The conversation moves from "What do I think?" to "What can I do?" It's both humbling and liberating.

When I started at IDEO in 2001, it was a part of the culture that every once in a while a group of designers would take a break from their client work and take on a seemingly impossible brief and see what they could do with it in a day. To this day, the most popular story about the organization—the so-called shopping cart video—is essentially an example of the practice. In brief, a 1999 episode of *Nightline* followed a set of about thirty multidisciplinary IDEO designers, a diverse but well-coordinated team, who were given a week to "reinvent" the shopping cart.

It's not surprising that this video, which is shown in business schools around the world, still elicits so much interest from people who see it and want to come to IDEO to work. The combination of an impossible task and the "do it in a day" time frame forces the very best of a culture to come forward. That's why impatience is such a virtue. The pressure to do something catalyzes a sense of community that is more collaborative and more helpful than the kinds of things you see in everyday culture. It is not singular to IDEO and can be reproduced anywhere with the right kind of goal and the right kind of constraints.

Creation Makes Community

Not far from the upstate farm town I live in, there's a small shop that carries antique quilts. I recently stopped in to peruse their stock, searching for something specific among the faded quilted blankets that hung from rods on the wall or were stacked on shelves and in bureaus around the space.

Finally, on the lowest shelf, almost purposely tucked away and out of sight, I found it: a multicolored quilt, assembled from what looked like scraps of fabric in all shapes and in all types—denim, chambray, even bits of felt—with a broad, rough stitching. The owner, a small, talkative man, looked surprised: "Oh, you're interested in rag quilts."

Rag quilts may not be as detailed or fine as many quilts, but they have a beauty of a different kind. They are the work of not one skilled quilter, but rather a small collection of women who came together—often from distant towns. They'd come bearing bits and scraps of fabric, puzzling them together, fingers rapidly moving, to assemble a completed blanket. As I gazed at that quilt in cold winter light, knowing its origins, it seemed like one of the most beautiful things I'd ever seen.

Pioneer women in the West used to travel hours to gather together for quilting bees; the goal was to stitch a quilt together in a day, something that might typically take weeks or more. It was an act of collective creation. It's also an act of creation that inspired important conversation.

"You know these quilts were often the backbone of the community," the shop owner said as I looked at it. It would be enigmatic, if I didn't know exactly what he meant. Many who study these kinds of "bees"—and there are many types: sewing bees, quilting bees, even barn bees—talk about how the conversations that happened over the work shared essential and much-needed information. Sometimes gossip, but more often far more critical information: health and medical tips for women and children; discussions of which households had been hit by the influenza; and other concerns of town and the community.

A lot of this community conversation and collective bonding can be attributed to the mesmeric distraction of quilting, which is similar to the knitting practice we talked about in creative listening. But the sense of collectivity continued long after the quilts were done. In the 1800s, the very women who made the rag quilt in my hands had organized to stop the rebuilding of the local tavern after it burned down. They were tired of losing their husbands to the drunken and violent establishment every night, leaving the town a dry town—or at least a town of "cabinet drinkers"—to this day.

In almost every culture there is a tradition of neighboring farmers coming together to harvest a field or build an outbuilding; whether it's a barn raising or an Estonian *talgup*—communal farm work—assembling to help each other and to make something is a real and consistent human behavior. And we need to tap into that now more than ever.

I worked with Surgeon General Vivek Murthy on a project about anxiety in America and the root cause—isolation. Scholar Julianne Holt-Lundstad, who studies the impact of loneliness, told us that loneliness and isolation literally wear down the body; people who are lonely seem to age quicker and are more physically vulnerable. Her research suggests that people in isolation are experiencing the health effect of the equivalent of smoking more than fifteen cigarettes a day. Isolation is a chronic condition—even more so amid a pandemic—in America and just doing something together can be a cure.

Right now, in New York there are LGBTQ knitting circles, which are community alternatives to bar culture. There are new salons where part of the evening's discussion centers around making the meal. Making something together promises a future and promises an outcome, and that shifts the tone of the conversation, which becomes in itself positive and productive. Sometimes you just have to make up something to make.

Try, Not Talk

There is another critical reason to shift from conversation to creation to making. It's often simply referred to as "analysis paralysis": the more we talk about something, the less certain we become about what to do about it.

Ironically, this kind of stalled moment can be a product of the very best exploratory conversations. Once we have looked at a problem or a topic from many different perspectives and explored many different solutions, it can be harder to decide upon the right path forward. Almost every part of this book is about supplying tools to maneuver through moments when conversations go wrong, but what happens when they leave you uncertain about what to do next?

That's when you need to try, not talk.

I always come back to the work of Antanas Mockus, the former mayor of Bogotá, who inherited a city rife with troubles and gradually reinvented it. My true and deep admiration of Mockus was born out of his powerful habit of not talking and just trying things.

My favorite example is the mayor's solution to traffic fatalities in Bogotá. The city had one of the highest pedestrian death rates—if you've ever been there, you'll know the traffic is intense and the relative lawlessness of the drivers is unique—and it had been in a long struggle about what to do. Most of the deaths occurred when pedestrians didn't keep to standard crosswalks and other designated foot traffic areas. Local traffic officers had issued high-fee tickets, but no one really took that seriously, and many considered the fees to be bribes.

Mockus and his team gave the problem considerable thought, reflecting on what really mattered most to Colombians: their pride. With little testing, and no research, Mockus decided to just try something: he replaced pedestrian traffic cops with mimes—you know, the silent clowns that everyone hates. There were about five hundred of them, placed at busy intersections; their sole job was to watch for violations and do what mimes know how to do best, make fun of the jaywalkers.

Over the next decade traffic fatalities dropped 50 percent.

The program was so successful that police officers and other law enforcement officers were given mime training, which they applied not just to traffic violations but other criminal activities. Furthermore, mimes spread; in fact, in my travels through Central and South America, it's not uncommon to find mimes—some in a pretty lame state, but still—at the corners of major intersections praising good behaviors, shaming the others.

There is an inventiveness and humor in Mockus's work, but what I find really inspiring was his continuing willingness to try something, to just put it out there and see. Some of his experiments failed—at one point he distributed cards with a thumbs-up, thumbs-down image to about 350,000 citizens of Bogotá so they could, in essence, begin to self-regulate shame or support the behavior of fellow citizens by holding the card up—appropriate side out—when they witnessed good or bad behavior. It sort of worked, but that was OK too. The point was that no amount of conjecture or conversation could have predicted the effectiveness of the solutions. It was an idea that just had to be tried to see if it worked.

We think big conversations should be followed by big actions, but the truth is, sometimes you just need to do anything rather than nothing. Look at the solutions and imagine: "What's the smallest way we could do this? What allows us to make the conversation manifest? Can we stop talking and start trying?"

Creative Connections

As my work at IDEO increasingly shifted away from the private sector toward the realm of government, philanthropy, and nonprofit, so too did we see the issues we were working on expand in size and scale. Suddenly our brief included issues like economic disparity, fair distribution of health care, climate change, and beyond. While much of the work to date had been about how to steward conversations within organizations to make change and create new things, suddenly the work was about stewarding conversations between multiple highly divergent organizations and types of organizations. This is where beginning to think about dialogue as a creative process really started to emerge for me.

Essential to the final piece of creative conversation, to creation, the actual manifestation of an idea, is a practice that is somewhat abhorrent to me, IDEO, and designers in general: networking. Networking is an essential aspect of much of the work many of us do, but in some ways the ideas of managing and navigating networks of people felt too willfully political and mercenary. "We just want to make things," we told ourselves, but we began to realize that making things wasn't possible in this large-scale space of systems change if we tried to do it alone. From this realization emerged an idea called creative connections—the idea that assembling networks of individuals and organizations could be itself a fundamentally creative act.

I encourage you to look at who else should be in a conversation, who else can help as fundamental to the idea of making something. Don't do it alone—yes—but, more important, think seriously about who needs to be in a conversation in order to make something happen. There are, in essence, two simple ways to begin to use creative connection as a means to help you build and create your future: the rule of firsts and taking a second.

THE RULE OF FIRSTS

There's a fairly well-known game people play called Six Degrees of Kevin Bacon—the idea is to go through a set of the people you know well; in turn, go through the people they know well and so on and so on until you find what level of separation you are from meeting Kevin Bacon. Essentially you can play that game with any well-known person and the winner is the one who has the fewest degrees of separation.

The question I find to be most valuable for any group of people who are assembling with the intention of creating something or moving a conversation beyond that room is: "Who might help who is one phone call away?"

This is what I call the Rule of Firsts and it's a useful tool to help make sure a conversation continues.

Whenever I'm with a group of people who are working on a specific area of exploration and who might be ready to think about how to make something happen, I do a simple Rule of

Firsts exercise. Ask the question, "Who could help that I could pick up the phone and call?" not just of yourself but of everyone in the room with you.

If you take five minutes to pause and reflect on this and write the names of people on cards, a whiteboard, or Post-its, what you find is the next set of participants to reach out to help think about how to take a conversation forward. Do this fast and in a generative way, almost like a very short brainstorm. It's not about who you know, it's about who you know who you think can help.

Sometimes what comes out of that list-making exercise is a set of new collaborators. You might even find people who are better able to take an idea forward than your group.

When I was at IDEO, before even starting work, often before planning project work on large problems, we do a brief round of the Rule of Firsts to see who might be useful, even just to help the conversation get off the ground. The practice was so easy and, in so many ways, so inspiring—we had friends we could find to help—that, little by little, creative connections became second nature to us.

TAKE A SECOND

I was once in a meeting with the chief marketing officer of a large retailer and key members of her team. We had just started in on the biggest idea when the executive interrupted us. She swung around to her team and asked, "OK, wait, who's not in the room right now that needs to hear this?"

They all did a mental tally and quickly identified a number of people who they felt should probably have been there. We stopped the meeting while they called their missing colleagues and they made their way to our office from their headquarters—mercifully only a few blocks away.

The meeting resumed from the beginning, but I remember thinking that I'd just witnessed one of the more inspirational moments of leadership in my whole career: a leader who knew that there were people who needed to be in a conversation because it was going to affect the work they did from then on out.

When you start to move from creative conversation to the act of creation it may be that the people in the room—those who've had the conversation—are not the people who can carry the ideas forward. Sometimes this has to do with the makeup of the room, people missing or overlooked. This can require a rethink. Maybe it's about all new people, but often it's about the addition of new voices and new skills, identifying the right continued collaborators.

But after that moment with the marketing officer, I understood the value of "take a second."

When you're creating a conversation or invited to one to help solve a problem and enact the solution, always invite someone along who is the "doer." The benefits of this are significant. The doer is in the conversation, they are a part of the idea, and they participate in the catalytic change a creative conversation can have. They are no longer the recipient of a task—the creation—but the participant in the development of the idea.

Preselecting the second is by far the easiest way to ensure creation. However, almost all important strategic conversations require added voices to make sure that they continue, and yet it's rare that I see time on an agenda devoted to identifying who else needs to be in the conversation to help expand it and move from talking to making.

In truth the minds that develop a new idea are not the same as the hands that can make it happen. This plays out on the organizational level as well. If you bring a diverse set of organizations together to work on a problem, that doesn't mean that you have the organizations in the room that can fulfill on that promise. It would be far better for that group to spend time working on what organization or player in the world is best suited to take an idea forward, in which case the last stage of a creative conversation might really be just to identify who is best to continue the work and how to draw them into the conversation.

So, whenever I explore the next steps of an expanding conversation and the move to creation, I build a list as broad and as expansive as it can be and then collectively look at that list and ask who needs to be in the conversation going forward. Once those individuals and organizations are identified, it's time to build a kind of conversation missionary team.

Make Conversation: The Sundance Film Lab

Michelle Satter is the founding director of the Sundance Directors and Screenwriters Lab, held annually at the Sundance Resort, the summer home of the Sundance Institute. For thirty-five years she has worked closely with Robert Redford, the founder of the Sundance Institute, and a committed staff to support almost every significant independent filmmaker—from Quentin Tarantino to Ryan Coogler and Dee Rees. Michelle has provided ongoing support to advance their work and ultimately jump-started their careers as filmmakers. Numerous artistic residencies gather artists in unique locations and provide them with time and space to develop their art, but few are as hands-on and focused as The Sundance Lab. It is both a conversation and an act of creation.

To qualify for the Directors Lab, you must have a strong version of the script you're developing and an idea of four or five critical and most challenging scenes that you would like to shoot in a workshop setting. If your script is accepted, you are assigned key collaborators as your crew: professional actors that you cast; and the production resources you will need in the weeks ahead. During each week, you film one or two scenes with a day of rehearsal, a day of shooting, and a day of editing. Then you're on to your next round with the feedback and insights of a group of creative advisers.

It's fast and it can be painful. When I went to observe a complex scene in rehearsal, the team was working through what felt like a straightforward heist scene until you realized that it was made complex by the need for continuous camera movement. I watched for hours as they worked through the extraordinarily complex choreography; the actors and crew were getting tired and visibly grumpy. When I left the shoot, it seemed like the task was impossible, so imagine my delight when I watched the film and that specific scene in a theater two years later. It was exhilarating.

At the same time filmmakers are going through a fairly frenzied pace scripting, rehearsing, filming, and editing these scenes, Michelle and the team of creative advisers are working through a thoughtful and deliberate process, a creative conversation that she developed unique to the lab. Every year, she builds a team of eight accomplished professionals to work with her alongside the directors. This team is typically composed of several directors, an editor, an actor, a screenwriter, and a cinematographer; all are well known in their field—famous, really.

Each of them observes one director's process for the first day of the week, and from that point onward, every morning before the day starts, that group gets together to discuss what they saw the day before and what that director could use some help on. They sit together in a circle in the middle of the room (observers like me sit off to the side).

Despite all the work that needs to happen in so little time, this meeting is a respite from that pace and that pressure. It's slow, it's open and critical, but it's kind and caring as well. The conversation is rigorous in focusing on what was witnessed in the work the day before and where help might be needed. The goal of that meeting is in fact exactly that, to find issues and offer help.

When the meeting ends, everyone heads out to do the day's work. Michelle and the creative adviser team will spend the day alongside the directors and their actors and crew. The conversation results in an almost immediate action, and the action leads to results within hours. For me, watching this meeting was a transformational experience. As a designer, I have worked with some of the most creative people in organizations around the world. But to be honest, when you see a meeting like this, you wish it was happening in your workplace every single morning. It was just unbelievably inspiring.

The lab is almost perfectly designed for creative conversation: it mixes the slow with the fast; there are rules of critique and the critics will be working side by side with the artists; there's a clear journey and a clear destination; oh, and it's in a pretty gorgeous and remote destination. For most of the people who attend, it's a unique life experience.

So there's a ton here for you to emulate. But let's pay closest attention now to how it embodies the most important parts of this book: it's about establishing a set of helpers, deciding when to stop talking and doing, and setting a plan for how the conversation will continue when it's over. It is built around and for the clear and collective goal to create something together. When was the last time that was your intention?

The very act of creation is a courageous, generous, and optimistic act. Perhaps the best way to forge new bonds, to build community and a common path, is with the simple but powerful act of creating, making conversation together.

Conversation Break:
Principles For Conversations in a Virtual World

Just as I was completing the book, I was asked by the Rockefeller Foundation to join them in looking at how they might redesign their convenings and gatherings. They have a truly stunning facility at Lake Como in northern Italy, and have used it historically to host powerful gatherings with remarkable people that make real change happen in the world, yet they thought they could do better.

A week after my first visit to Bellagio, the center was closed—all of northern Italy was closed due to a once-in-a-lifetime pandemic. Gradually, in the weeks that followed, other cities, workplaces, and communities found themselves "sheltered in place."

So while COVID-19 is new to us, plagues in some form have always occurred, and in fact they can prove to be good for conversation. *The Decameron* by Boccaccio is in fact the story of ten nobles sheltered in place—granted, in a castle—entertaining themselves by telling ten stories a day over ten days, not a bad way to pass the time.

For those of us not sheltered together in a castle, we simply moved our conversations online. Zoom meetings became the norm, FaceTime cocktail hours became the way we saw our friends, and life—sometimes awkwardly, sometimes seamlessly—slipped onto the screen. While the debate will continue for a long time on whether this kind of interaction can ever replace the warmth of in-person conversations, virtual conversations are now permanently embedded in our lives.

What follows are five principles for making conversations online.

1. ASSESS AND COMMIT . . . OR DON'T

Ask yourself if this is a conversation you should be in. Over the last decades we shifted into a "more is more" mentality, and an "always on" work style. That mentality doesn't translate well to remote work. I recently attended a two-day, nine-hour-a-day board meeting on Zoom that I would characterize as a crime against humanity.

For many of us, it is second nature to want to be in the room where the action takes place, but rethink that instinct. Start to self-assess and review the conversations you're normally in and

decide whether or not you need to be in them at all. This reflection, on whether you are absolutely material to the outcomes
of a conversation, is intended to benefit the conversation: the
more people that are involved in a virtual convening, the less
effective it is.

There is a personal benefit, too. Take the time to reassess
where you should be participating and where your participation
is less valuable, and you may end up making a better work life
for yourself. Take note, however, that if you are a sole voice of
difference in the "room," you absolutely need to be there. No
matter what, if you decide to participate, then take responsibility to own and commit to the work that comes out of that
conversation.

2. BREAK THE RULES, ALL OF THEM

This is not an in-person gathering, so don't treat it like one.
The challenge isn't a technical one, i.e., "let's get everyone on
Zoom." Instead, it's a question of what the ideal work and collaborative process is. You can entirely redesign the conversation
to best suit the new circumstances and the new opportunities.
Think, for instance, about length and timing. The chapter on
constraints is particularly relevant now.

So often, meetings, especially large convenings, are planned
weeks or months in advance and are about the scale of gathering. They're scheduled for people to be together for as long as
they possibly can.

Once you remove the pressure of a live gathering, a convening *can become anything*. Consider more sessions, but shorter
sessions. If it was previously a gathering of sixty people, consider

ten short sessions, with groups of just six, spread over two weeks. Think seriously about the rules of engagement and be deliberate about establishing them before going forward. The rules can be simple (how to signal who should be talking next) or more sophisticated and challenging (how long people have to make a point and how they might make it).

When you make your conversation virtual, all rules are on the table.

3. ADAPT THE MEDIUM TO THE WORK

We have more media platforms at our fingertips than just videoconferencing tools. If you break the rules about what a convening is, you can rethink your use of technology too.

The telephone is a remarkably elegant and intimate medium that allows for a kind of directness and openness that we don't have when we're face-to-face. People confess sins when they can't see people, people fall in love with people on late-night calls, people can think aloud (even close their eyes) when they aren't distracted by visual stimuli.

Using a Google Doc in real time can make editing and the related conversations feel as fulfilling as sitting face-to-face. I've had long afternoons working in a Google Doc with my editor. By the end of the day, it felt nearly as fulfilling as sitting together and talking about the book. Think about Donaree and her book group or a quilting circle: when you work together "in" a document, you are uniting over content and creating it together.

Use and tune different technologies for the kinds of "conversations" you make and don't be afraid to experiment with each. What's particularly powerful about letting more and varied media into your life is that it employs different voices, talents, and kinds of thinking that may not occur face-to-face.

4. AIM FOR SIMPLICITY AND ELEGANCE

In a virtual context, clarity, purpose, and simplicity matter more than ever. If it was hard to "cut someone off" before, then it's even harder now. It's not about eloquence, it's about elegance.

As always, a simple short story can help establish clarity around meaning when we have fewer physical and nonverbal cues to help us define and understand.

But remember: Is the story you're telling making a point? Is it making the point you want? Is it even a story? If you find yourself having to go back to your childhood to explain what happened to you yesterday, that's probably not an effective story. Go back to the conversation break on illuminations for inspiration on how to do this.

5. DESIGN HUMANS IN

In a virtual context, it's more important than ever to design with humor, joy, even love.

Take a moment to share fears, yes, but, maybe more important, take a moment to acknowledge what is good. I've been using new opening prompts—for instance, take a moment to share the one thing you would be in nature if you could be anything. That kind of opening question actually triggers serotonin. It may feel dorky, but it works. Turns out, feeling dorky is part of being human.

Go back to the tips and tricks throughout the book and

see how they can help. Building pauses into conversations can really help in the virtual context. Ask people to write what they're thinking for a short moment, and then share that with the virtual group. Or ask them to draw a diagram or share a photo. We may be mediated by a machine but you can still experience what it means to be human.

Design in humor, express gratitude for results, contemplate nature, or just pause and breathe.

A Concluding Reflection

Writing can be such a struggle as you try to shape the things you see, feel, and think into something coherent and powerful. Sometimes you have to put the pen down (or the keyboard aside) to be able to reflect on what you've learned. As this book goes to press, in the summer of the COVID-19 pandemic, I keep thinking back on a conversation I had with a Dewey student. At the end of our phone interview, she wanted to ask me a question. Of course I said yes. She proceeded. "So you've been out there and experienced all these people having all kinds of amazing conversations, do you feel cured?"

The question surprised me. Because it was so couched in the language of trauma, I instinctively flinched from the phone. But I realized the question was absolutely right. I had in fact entered into the research and writing of this book in a state of trauma. I had begun with a heavy heart, believing that we as a culture, as members of organizations, had begun to fail at making conversation, and I wasn't convinced we could ever recover. Researching the topic for this book had become my way,

I realize now, of proving my theory wrong. So as I sat there in silence for a moment, pondering her question, it dawned on me: Yes, I had been "cured." I had come to see we could still make creative conversations happen—as this book makes clear, they are happening in lots of places already.

In writing the book I had been in the extremely privileged position of seeking out unique and powerful examples of situations in which people had somehow overcome some form of collective or individual hardship to generate difficult, remarkable, and often joyful conversations. I use the word *privileged* because daily life doesn't always give us opportunities to experience moments like this, especially if we're mainly exposed to TV news or noisy social media platforms. Unfortunately, conversations that devolve into conflict, aggression, and disrespect are more "newsworthy" than good creative conversations, so that's what we experience. And that's what some people have come to expect.

But it doesn't have to be so.

As shelter-in-place and economic shutdowns have enveloped most of the planet in 2020, there was still plenty of noise and strife and confusion, but there were also moments of profound connection, resilience, and creativity. And there was also a longing for what might be lost. Sure, some of us missed dining out at our favorite restaurants, getting regular haircuts, and just wandering around in crowded marketplaces. But what did we miss the most? What do we truly need to feel alive? Making conversations that matter. Gathering with others who cause us to think differently, to grow and to learn. This is the privilege that we all should have access to.

And now we can all take personal responsibility for giving our attention to, and sharing stories of, people who have been creative in their conversations, who have made change happen, and have persevered. We can become conversation starters ourselves. This is the counternarrative we need to bring to life because these conversations *hold the key to a cure*.

ACKNOWLEDGMENTS

First, a thank-you to the people who literally made this book happen. Debbe Stern, who recognized that there might be teeth to this topic. Christy Fletcher, my agent, who emailed literally just after seeing my talk on designing dialogue and said, "Maybe there's a book here?" The team at HarperCollins, but especially Hollis Heimbouch. I remember sitting down with her the first time we met and feeling that she had a clearer vision for this book than I did. Thanks also to Keith Knueven, who worked closely with the HarperCollins design team to build a cover we all loved. My research assistant, Hannah Rudin, who still worries I got it wrong. Special thanks to Mark Lotto, a combination therapist and writing teacher, who worked alongside me from proposal through the final chapter. Don't even try to write a book without him. Shoshana, thanks for pointing the way to Mark.

Then there are all the friends who had to live through years of me talking about talking about things. My husband, who, when he read it, was like, "Um, I really didn't need to read it, you've told me all this." Whitney Mortimer, who was with me on the first hike high on some mountain when the idea first came up. We had to stop every five minutes so I could write something down. My friends who for two years have heard me talk about either creativity in conversation or how hard it was to write: Tim Marshall, Janet Roitman, Roshi Givechi, Jocelyn Wyatt, Tom Eich, S. Quinn, Chal Pivik, Deborah Marton, Justine Nagen, Beth Viner, Zia Khan, Dawn Laguens, Philip Himburg, Dominique Bluhdorn, John Wotowicz, Shanelle Matthews, Diane Morris, and pretty much anyone else I talked to over the last couple years. More than a few of them let me "experiment on them" to see how it worked.

Thanks to all the people who have been icons and models of good conversation and in many ways inspired me to write this book, many of whom are in the book. David Kelley, Bill Moggridge, George Papandreou, Vivek Murthy, Lisa Kron, Mary Gentile, Courtney E. Martin, Michelle Satter, Andrea Lein, the students of the John Dewey Academy, Pat Mitchell, Joan Kane, and of course my mom, June Dust. Some of you are mentors, some co-conspirators, and many I'm lucky enough to call friend.

It's going to be impossible to capture all the co-conspirators at IDEO or in the world who have been designing conversations with me or on their own over the years, but here's a try: Anna Silverstein, Christopher Hibma, Daniel Neville-Rehbehn, Ashley Powell-Sommer (you four, plus some others mentioned earlier, were my first fellow "dialogue designers"), Diana Rhoten, Ingrid Fetell-Lee, Zorana Pringle, Wendy Woon, Paul Bennet, Ellie Grossman, Elif Gokcidem, Amelia Winger-Bearskin, Kamal Sinclair, Sam Utne, Molly Utne, Sarah Reinhoff, Tina Roth-Eisenberg, Patrice Martin, Brian Walker, David Kirchoff, Keri Putnam, Michael Hendrickson, Ann Kim, Nili Metuki, Alex Gallafent, Erin Henkel, Sandy Speicher, Dana Cho, Kourtney Bitterly, Ilya Prokopoff, Jeff Hitner, Eddie Shiomi, Lawrence Abrahamson, Njoki Gitahi, Albert Lee, Ambika Nigam, Amy Leventhal, Anette Diefenthaler, Brendon Boyle, Gitte Jonsdatter, Kate Lydon, Margaret Kessler, Dan Wandry, Mark Buchalter, Suzanne Howard, Liz Danzico, Loren Mayor.

Finally, thanks to so many of my fellow colleagues at IDEO, clients, and collaborators whom I may not have named.

NOTES

CHAPTER 1: **COMMITMENT**

21 "who were not previously their friends": Timothy Snyder, *On Tyranny: Twenty Lessons from the Twentieth Century* (New York: Tim Duggan Books, 2017), 84.

22 "stand up and speak your mind": Mary C. Gentile, *Giving Voice to Values: How to Speak Your Mind When You Know What's Right* (New York: The McGraw-Hill Companies, Inc., 2010).

23 people we trust: Larisa Heiphetz, Elizabeth S. Spelke, Paul L. Harris, and Mahzarin R. Banaji, "The Development of Reasoning about Beliefs: Fact, Preference, and Ideology," *Journal of Experimental Social Psychology* 49, no. 3 (May 2013): 559–65, doi.org/10.1016/j.jesp.2012.09.005

23 helping children form beliefs: Ibid.

24 they don't act out but rather fall inward: Sherry Turkle, *Reclaiming Conversation: The Power of Talk in a Digital Age* (New York: Penguin Books, 2015).

25 higher education and the liberal arts: Greg Lukianoff and Jonathan Haidt, *The Coddling of the American Mind: How Good Intentions and Bad Ideas Are Setting Up a Generation for Failure* (New York: Penguin Press, 2018).

28 "Well, they're my species": *Harold and Maude*, directed by Hal Ashby, Mildred Lewis and Colin Higgins Productions, Inc. and Paramount Pictures, 1971.

35 "sympathy and empathy with patients and family," and "to inspire hope": Mayo Clinic Health System — Eau Claire, "Mission, Vision, and Value Statements," accessed August 26, 2019, https:// mayoclinichealthsystem.org/locations/eau-claire/about-us/mission -vision-and-value-statements.

39 "whatever you see can inspire you": *The September Issue*, directed by R. J. Cutler, A&E Indie Films and Actual Reality Pictures, 2009.

CHAPTER 2: CREATIVE LISTENING

45 says one teaching manual: Michael Linsin, "Should Students Raise Their Hand in Small Groups?" Smart Classroom Management, last modified February 14, 2015, https://www.smartclassroommanagement .com/2015/02/14/should-students-raise-their-hand-in-small-groups/.

46 tingly sort of attentiveness: Theo Tsaousides, "Why Are We Scared of Public Speaking?" *Psychology Today*, November 27, 2017, https://www .psychologytoday.com/us/blog/smashing-the-brainblocks/201711/why -are-we-scared-public-speaking.

47 a deceptively simple concept—was released: Karal Ann Marling, *As Seen on TV: The Visual Culture of Everyday Life in the 1950s* (Cambridge: Harvard University Press, 1996).

47 the realm of channel surfing: Mary Bellis, "The Television Remote Control: A Brief History," ThoughtCo, last modified September 20, 2019, https://www.thoughtco.com/history-of-the-television-remote -control-1992384.

48 without missing a television show: Jason Plautz, "The Toddlers' Truce: Why You Couldn't Watch British TV at 6pm Until 1957," *Mental Floss*, February 16, 2012, https://www.mentalfloss.com/article/30006 /toddlers-truce-why-you-couldnt-watch-british-tv-6pm-until-1957.

49 person-centered therapy: Raymond J. Corsini and Raymond Danny Wedding, *Current Psychotherapies* (Boston: Cengage Learning, 2013), 95–150.

50 "help you stay focused": Mrs. Wolfe's Art and Health, "Active Listening," Bulb, last modified November 23, 2014, https://www .bulbapp.com/u/active-listening.

50 "emphasis on parts of the message": Bold Networking, "Active Listening to Grow Rapport," accessed December 9, 2019, https:// boldnetworking.com/active-listening-2/.

50 A sample: Anupam Guha, "ELIZA/Doctor Program," class report, University of Maryland, 2012, https://www.cs.umd.edu/class/fall2012 /cmsc828d/oldreportfiles/guha1.pdf.

53 to build a mindful listening practice: Nancy Chick, "Doodling & Knitting," The Mindful PhD, last modified January 22, 2014, https:// my.vanderbilt.edu/themindfulphd/2014/01/doodling-knitting/.

55 "is always speaking": QuakerSpeak, "How to Listen for a Leading," YouTube video, 6:53, May 18, 2016, https://www.youtube.com /watch?v=K9D-RQ7Xr5Q&feature=youtu.be.

57 preparation, incubation, illumination, and verification: Simone M. Ritter and Ap Dijksterhuis, "Creativity—the Unconscious Foundations of the Incubation Period," *Frontiers in Human Neuroscience* 8, no. 215 (April 2014), doi:10.3389/fnhum.2014.00215.

65 some gossiping may actually be good for us: Tania Lombrozo, "Why Do We Gossip?" *NPR*, May 23, 2016, https://www.npr.org/sections /13.7/2016/05/23/479128912/the-origins-of-gossip.

CHAPTER 3: CLARITY

77 "we may have simply passed over": Meara Sharma, "How the Loss of Vivid, Exacting Language Diminishes Our World," *Washington Post*, December 8, 2017, https://www.washingtonpost.com/outlook /how-the-loss-of-vivid-exacting-language-diminishes-our-world /2017/12/08/4630e920-c265-11e7-84bc-5e285c7f4512_story.html.

92 Japanese literary tradition: "Haiku," Literary Devices, accessed December 10, 2019, https://literarydevices.net/haiku/.

92 describe their businesses in a haiku format: Shané Schutte, "Can You Describe Your Growing Business in a Haiku?" *Real Business*, June 18, 2018, https://realbusiness.co.uk/describing-business-in-a-haiku/.

93 business leadership in the haiku form: Kellogg Insight, "You Sent Us Business Haiku, Here Are Our Favorites," Kellogg School of Management, May 7, 2016, https://insight.kellogg.northwestern.edu /article/you-sent-us-business-haiku-here-are-our-favorites.

104 albeit continuously revised: Henry M. Robert, Daniel H. Honemann, and Thomas J. Balch, with contributions from Daniel E. Seabold and

Shmuel Gerber, *Robert's Rules of Order*, Rev. ed. (New York: Public Affairs, 2011).

CHAPTER 4: CONTEXT

107 "quality without a name": Christopher Alexander, *The Timeless Way of Being* (Oxford, United Kingdom: Oxford University Press, 1979), 123.

113 trying to memorize something: Wadsworth Cengage Learning, "Kinds of Mnemonics," *Essential Study Skills*, accessed August 26, 2019, http://college.cengage.com/collegesurvival/wong/essential_study/6e/assets/students/protected/wong_ch06_in-depthmnemonics.html.

113 spaces we inhabit: Robinson Meyer, "In the Brain, Memories Are Inextricably Tied to Place," *The Atlantic*, August 12, 2014, https://www.theatlantic.com/technology/archive/2014/08/in-the-brain-memories-are-inextricably-tied-to-place/375969/.

114 patterns historically found in space: Christopher Alexander, Sara Ishikawa, Murray Silverstein, Max Jacobson, Ingrid Fiksdahl-King, and Shlomo Angel, *A Pattern Language: Towns, Buildings, Construction* (Oxford, United Kingdom: Oxford University Press, 1977).

116 the whole building was constructed around steps: The New School, "Stairs Take University Center," New School News, October 29, 2013, https://blogs.newschool.edu/news/2013/10/stairs-take-university-center/.

123 goes out the door: Marie Kondo, *The Life-Changing Magic of Tidying Up: The Japanese Art of Decluttering and Organizing* (Berkeley, CA: Ten Speed Press, 2014).

124 decision fatigue: Trina N. Dao, "Office Clutter and Its Influence: Assessing Engagement, Satisfaction, Tension, Stress, and Emotional Exhaustion" (2019), College of Science and Health Theses and Dissertations, 294, https://via.library.depaul.edu/csh_etd/294.

128 deeply in sync: Sian Beilock, *How the Body Knows Its Mind: The Surprising Power of the Physical Environment to Influence How You Think and Feel* (New York: Atria Books, 2015).

130 "the divinity incarnate in man": Carl G. Jung, *Memories, Dreams, Reflections* (New York: Knopf Doubleday Publishing Group, 2011), 335.

132 psychoanalytic practice: Nathan Kravis, *On the Couch: A Repressed*

History of the Analytic Couch from Plato to Freud (Cambridge: The MIT Press, 2017).

133 athletes gather to help build energy: Jeff Sutherland, "The Origins of the Daily Standup," ScrumInc., September 26, 2014, http://scruminc .com/origins-daily-standup/.

139 in the Swiss Alps: SDG, "Voyage into Silence: Interview with Philip Gröning," Decent Films, accessed August 26, 2019, http://decentfilms .com/articles/groning.

139 unique life of this monastic order: Philip French, "Into Great Silence," *The Guardian*, December 31, 2006, https://www.theguardian.com/film /2006/dec/31/worldcinema.documentary?CMP=Share_iOSApp_Other.

140 just too uncomfortable: Lucas Reilly, "The Story Behind John Cage's *4'33*"," *Mental Floss*, November 6, 2017, http://mentalfloss.com /article/59902/101-masterpieces-john-cages-433.

143 taking a moment of silence: Jill Suttie, "Four Ways Music Strengthens Social Bonds," *Greater Good Magazine*, January 15, 2015, https:// greatergood.berkeley.edu/article/item/four_ways_music_strengthens _social_bonds.

CHAPTER 5: CONSTRAINTS

145 "accept change": Mara Cristina Caballero, "Academic Turns City into a Social Experiment," *Harvard Gazette*, March 11, 2004, https://news .harvard.edu/gazette/story/2004/03/academic-turns-city-into-a-social -experiment/.

145 executive named Alex Osborn: American Association of Advertising Agencies, "Alex Osborn, the Father of Brainstorming," 4A's, accessed August 26, 2019, https://www.aaaa.org/timeline-event/74179/.

145 methodology behind creativity and design: Alex F. Osborn, *Applied Imagination: Principles and Procedures of Creative Thinking* (New York: Scribner, 1963).

146 foster creativity and collaboration: J. William Pfeiffer, *Pfeiffer & Company Library of Theories and Models: Management*, 2nd edition, vol. 26 (San Francisco: Jossey-Bass/Pfeiffer, 1998), http://home.snu .edu/~jsmith/library/body/v26.pdf.

147 and other formal settings: Henry M. Robert, Daniel H. Honemann, and Thomas J. Balch, with contributions from Daniel E. Seabold and

Shmuel Gerber, *Robert's Rules of Order*, Rev. ed. (New York: Public Affairs, 2011).

147   or the Socratic method: Lou Marinoff, "The Structure and Function of a Socratic Dialogue," Filosofia Prática, accessed August 26, 2019, https://sites.google.com/site/entelequiafilosofiapratica/aconselhamento-filosofico-1/the-structure-and-function-of-a-socratic-dialogue-by-lou-marinoff.

147   competitive debate teams: *Fast Talk*, directed by Debra Tolchinsky, Cross X Productions, 2011.

148   "responsive classroom": Chip Wood, "Schoolwide Rules Creation," Responsive Classroom, November 1, 2005, https://www.responsiveclassroom.org/schoolwide-rules-creation/.

156   avoid crisis thinking: Adam Eason, "The Science of Silence: Why Silence Is So Good for Your Brain," last modified May 3, 2018, https://www.adam-eason.com/science-silence/.

156   pressure to discuss and act: Idun Haugan, "Silence as a Superpower," *Norwegian SciTech News*, October 18, 2016, https://norwegianscitechnews.com/2016/10/silence-as-a-superpower/.

156   peak again in the early evening: Daniel H. Pink, *When: The Scientific Secrets of Perfect Timing* (New York: Riverhead Books, 2018).

157   politician James Shields: Julia Davis, "The Time Abe Lincoln and a Rival Almost Dueled," *Mental Floss*, September 18, 2014, http://mentalfloss.com/article/12382/time-abraham-lincoln-and-political-rival-almost-dueled-island.

157   The Code Duello: "About Hamilton-Burr Code Duello 1804," PiratedDocuments.com, accessed August 26, 2019, https://www.piratedocuments.com/hamilton-burr-code-duello/.

158   the rules have shifted and evolved: Ed Grabianowski, "How Duels Work," HowStuffWorks.com, published June 22, 2005, https://people.howstuffworks.com/duel2.htm.

158   even nicked an opponent: Chris Hutcheson and Brett McKay, "Man Knowledge: An Affair of Honor - The Duel," Art of Manliness, last updated November 2, 2018, https://www.artofmanliness.com/articles/man-knowledge-an-affair-of-honor-the-duel/.

163   visitors could actually try it out: Sarah Kennedy, "Notes on Yoko Ono's *White Chess Set*," *Inside/Out*, July 14, 2015, https://www.moma.org/explore/inside_out/2015/07/14/notes-on-yoko-onos-white-chess-set/.

169 entertain them with some form of oratory: Georges Duby, "The Courtly Model," in *A History of Women in the West: Silence of the Middle Ages Volume II*, ed. Christiane Klapisch-Zuber (Cambridge, MA: Harvard University Press, 1992), 250-266.

170 without it touching the ground: Andrew Fluegelman, *The New Games Book* (New York: Dolphin Books, 1979).

CHAPTER 6: CHANGE

173 "from the same source": Jad Abumrad, host, *Dolly Parton's America* (podcast), October 3, 2019, accessed November 18, 2019, https://www .npr.org/podcasts/765024913/dolly-parton-s-america.

181 "spiritually cleansed eyes": James Harpur, *The Pilgrim Journey: A History of Pilgrimage in the Western World* (New York: BlueBridge, 2016), 6.

181 "The Pilgrimage to Freedom": Stanford University, "Prayer Pilgrimage for Freedom," King Encyclopedia, accessed October 2, 2019, https://kinginstitute.stanford.edu/encyclopedia/prayer -pilgrimage-freedom.

183 "a notable rise in book clubs": Henry Alford, "Book Clubs Get Especially Clubby," *New York Times*, May 16, 2019, https://www .nytimes.com/2019/05/16/books/insider-niche-book-clubs-literaryswag.html; Gracy Olmstead, "Finding Community in a Book Club," *The American Conservative*, March 5, 2018, https://www .theamericanconservative.com/articles/finding-community-in-a-book -club/.

185 Let's look at Casper's podcast: Hannah Chanatry, "In a Harry Potter Podcast, a Search for Meaning in the Secular Through the Sacred," WBUR, last modified December 12, 2018, https://www.wbur.org /artery/2018/12/12/harry-potter-sacred-text-podcast.

185 have a Harry Potter book: "500 Million Harry Potter Books Have Now Been Sold Worldwide," *Pottermore*, February 1, 2018, https:// www.wizardingworld.com/news/500-million-harry-potter-books -have-now-been-sold-worldwide.

190 actively reviled: Alexandra Duncan, "Mierle Laderman Ukeles Artist Overview and Analysis," TheArtStory.org, accessed October 28, 2019, https://www.theartstory.org/artist/ukeles-mierle-laderman/.

190 tension between city workers and city residents: Nagle, Robin. "A Filthy History: When New Yorkers Lived Knee-Deep in Trash," interview by Hunter Oatman-Stanford, *Collectors Weekly*, June 24, 2013, https://www.collectorsweekly.com/articles/when-new-yorkers -lived-knee-deep-in-trash/.

190 and its sanitation workers: Randy Kennedy, "An Artist Who Calls the Sanitation Department Home," *New York Times*, September 21, 2016, https://nyti.ms/2cRzQvQ.

191 making their lives better: Patricia C. Phillips, with contributions from Tom Finkelpearl, Larissa Harris, Lucy Lippard, and Laura Raicovich *Mierle Laderman Ukeles: Maintenance Art* (New York: Prestel, 2016).

200 oxytocin: Gretchen Reynolds, "The 'Love Hormone' as Sports Enhancer," *New York Times*, November 21, 2012, https://well.blogs .nytimes.com/2012/11/21/the-love-hormone-as-sports-enhancer/.

CHAPTER 7: CREATE

201 "both the maker and the destination": Frederic Brussat and Mary Ann Brussat, directors, "Viewer's Guide to *The Day After*," educational resource, Cultural Information Service, 1983.

203 concerns about pollution: Rainer Nõlvak and Eva Truuverk, "Inspirational Instigators," interview by Let's Do It world staff, Let's Do It World, August 13, 2018, https://www.worldcleanupday.org /news/2018/08/13/inspirational-instigators.

203 in a single day: Helena Läks, "Estonia Leading a World Cleanup Day — Staying Stubborn and Uniting People," *Let's Do It! World Newsletter*, April 7, 2017, https://www.letsdoitworld.org/2017/04 /estonia-leading-world-cleanup-day-staying-stubborn-uniting-people/.

206 assemble a completed blanket: Angela Mitchell, "Quilting Bees for a Quilting Adventure," *Blueprint Quilting* (blog), April 29, 2018, https:// shop.mybluprint.com/quilting/article/quilting-bees/.

206 other concerns of town: Sherwood Smith, "The Quilting Bee Then and now," *Book View Cafe* (blog), August 19, 2012, http://bookviewcafe.com /blog/2012/08/19/the-quilting-bee-then-and-now/.

207 alternatives to bar culture: Britta Lokting, "Trading the Noisy Gay Bar Scene for the Knitting Circle," *New York Times*, June 7, 2019, https://

www.nytimes.com/2019/06/07/nyregion/knitting-gay-men.html
?login=smartlock&auth=login-smartlock.

208 traffic fatalities in Bogotá: Mara Cristina Caballero, "Academic Turns
City into a Social Experiment," *Harvard Gazette*, March 11, 2004,
https://news.harvard.edu/gazette/story/2004/03/academic-turns-city
-into-a-social-experiment/.

ABOUT THE AUTHOR

Fred Dust is a former senior partner and global managing director for the design firm IDEO.

Fred works at the intersection of business, society, and creativity. As a designer, author, educator, consultant, trustee, and adviser to social and business leaders, he is one of the world's most original thinkers, applying the craft and optimism of human-centered design to the intractable challenges we face today. Most recently, he has been investigating new ways to ignite constructive dialogue in a climate of widespread polarization, cynicism, and disruption.

Fred is a frequently requested speaker, adviser, and lecturer. He currently serves on the board of trustees for the Sundance Institute, the board of directors for NPR, and the board of directors at the New School. He was a founder and trustee for IDEO.org, IDEO's nonprofit that designs solutions to global poverty. He lectures widely on various topics, including design methodology, future trends, and social innovation.

Fred writes frequently for publications such as *Fast Company*, *Metropolis*, and *Rotman* magazine. His books include *Extra Spatial* (Chronicle Books, 2003), which discusses the design of spaces, and *Eyes Open: New York* and *Eyes Open: London* (Chronicle Books, 2008), city guides that view exceptional experiences through an urban lens.